INDIA BOOKVARSITY
LOTUS CHOICES
Editor: Mahendra Kulasrestha

COMPLETE BOOK OF

Hindu Gods and Goddesses

Edward Moor

All the Gods,
Goddesses, Demigods,
Scriptures, Sects, Symbols, etc.,
of the World's Most
Philosophical, People-oriented,
Multi-sided, Non-violent,
Cheer-cultured, Religious Family Group

Published by
Lotus Press Publishers & Distributors

COMPLETE BOOK OF
HINDU GODS AND GODDESSES

By
Edward Moor

Illustrated by
Mr. Haughton
Royal Academy

Source: ***The Hindu Pantheon,***
***The Court of All the Gods*;**
by Edward Moor, F.R.S.,
Published by J.J. Johnson, St. Paul's Church Yard,

London, 1810

Complete Book of
Hindu Gods and Goddesses

Edition—2026
ISBN: 978-81-8382-245-9 (HB)

Published by:
Lotus Press Publishers & Distributors
4735/22, Prakash Deep Building,
Ansari Road, Darya Ganj, New Delhi-110002
Ph.: 41325510, 9811838000
E-mail: lotuspress1984@gmail.com
www.lotuspress.co.in

Printed & Published: **Lotus Press Publishers & Distributors, New Delhi**

Editorspeak

Religion as Culture

Once when a few years ago, a friend of mine, Pradeep Mandav, to name him as an expression of gratitude, while discussing matters of religion, commented that Religion may be whatever it is, it is also Culture—which struck me with a force that changed my thinking in a very fundamental way.

Religion and God/gods have acquired a different shape everywhere in the world, and also its importance – somewhere more, somewhere less, and in some places not at all – has varied in remarkable ways. These have been non-violent and violent – too killing in some of them, others as also themselves (read Karen Armstrong's books on Abraham's three religions)–, anti-idolists and idol - worshippers with gusto, simple ideas-manipulators and highly philosophical, swinging around a long range of speculations and possibilities. Well, the problems galore of life and 'sufferings' starting from one's unexpected entry into the phenomenon called 'Life', to a great extent made such endeavours necessary to sustain a sense of well-being and usefulness in an otherwise dark and debilitating scenario.

I regard India as the best in the whole family of world religions, though I myself prefer to be a non-religious person. We always had many religions—not one prophet, one book, one symbol, doors closed affair—; professedly non-violent and tolerant — though winning people the world over without the help of a sword—; **essentially philosophical and intellectual; believers in God as also non-believers; inventors of the till-date-considered-highest concept of Atman and Brahman** (Paul Deussen and others underlined it over a century ago); and also, what is important in the context of the present book full of gods and goddesses of both genders, shapes and hues, serving the needs of the vast masses of people, poor and sick people, protecting them, curing and healing them, and cheering them with music and song in temples big and small, and through ceremonies and festivals spread all over the year.

This is the beautiful, wonderful, bountiful, cultural aspect of religion, Indian, with which the present editor is chiefly concerned, if not the other prevalent religions.

The British who came to India to conquer, were Christians, who, having always lived under the cross-generated gloom and one-book monotony, were not aware of the variety and richness — and also the thought-provoking philosophy of its central scriptures, were simply overwhelmed and, in addition to carrying out their everyday tasks in the service of the East India Company, many of them devoted to the exploration and study of Indian culture in its various aspects, forming scholarly societies not only in the major cities of India but in their own countries also. They researched, wrote, published and promoted, thus contributing as well as changing the scholarly-literary climate of the world tremendously.

The temples of India, the gods and goddesses smiling in them, and the devotional activities were great attractions to many Englishmen working in various capacities in the country. Much is not known about Edward Moor but he seems to have travelled widely, including China, about which strange land he makes some interesting comments, but for a major part, on the evidence of this book, he stayed in Poona during the later part of Peshwa supremacy. He studied the current aspects of Hindu religion astonishingly extensively, visiting, meeting, collecting material, including a large number of statues, idols, paintings, etc., most of which he later on donated to London and Indian museums.

The book he wrote, the present one—an earlier one is also mentioned—is a fairly big one, of 2 lakh words, and published exactly 200 years ago, in 1810, in London. It is very comprehensive, covering most aspects of the subject in careful detail; I find it surprising. The classifications are correct even by today's measures. And the illustrations are mind-boggling: since photography was not easy in those times, he made these done by a Royal Society artist.

In over a hundred pages, over 500 big and miniature drawings are given — may be even more. Surmising that Moor may have taken two-plus decades to research, collect, pen down and publish, the work presents a picture of Hindu religion in about 250 years old times, which gives it a special scholarly value.

To do it in the modern edition, I've condensed it considerably, rearranged the chapters, and drastically cut the number of pictures, selecting the representative ones only. Still, I believe, it is most useful and gives a complete picture of Hindu religion and its deities. I feel, every Indian should give it a reading; I was myself surprised by the extra information he gave in the whole version. He tells that at least two more Trimurtis, other than the Elephanta one, were found around Mumbai—the one that appears in the pages of this book is from the latter. The temple at the Malabar Hill's southern tip is described in interesting detail—of which nothing now remains—, where the Peshwa Raghoba acrobated regularly in a specially religious way.

The author is, rather unexpectedly, very appreciative of the place of honour given to cow in Hindu culture, and hoped that after some time the West will also accept it—though it has not happened till date. He analyses in quite some detail the use of cow-dung in Indian homes, including the kitchens, for the purpose of cleaning and cooling, but regrets that the British were changing it thoughtlessly. Similarly, his comparisons of our deities, etc., with the Greek and Latin idols, indicating that they were copies of the Hindu ones, are also quite convincing, and in some cases, very striking—though in the present edition, much of that material has been left out for the sake of saving space.

Edward Moor seems to have read whatever was available on the subject in English at that time, and regrets that he didn't know Sanskrit, and himself collected whatever he could lay his hands upon—his home would have been a veritable museum occupying much space. His classifications and conclusions are very pertinent, strikingly exact and correct, unbiased, and at times presenting a fresh angle to an otherwise difficult subject. I am specially pleased that I have the opportunity to present his work to the new generation after so long a time.

I am sure it is a significant addition to INDIA BOOK-VARSITY series.

Brahma, the Creator

Authorspeak

An Extraordinary People

It having fallen to my lot to visit, in very early life, the extraordinary people whose mythology I here endeavour to explain, and to remain among them, in situations frequently favorable to the acquisition of information, I take the liberty of offering to the public this work, the result of my observations and inquiries.

During an intercourse of many years, with natives of almost every description, I often, in conversation on interesting topics, found myself at a loss in comprehending certain terms and allusions, and in seeking what I required; and frequently experienced the utility of pictures and visible objects in directing me in both, hence I began to collect pictures and images, which in the progress of years, being particularly valuable as a selection, have accumulated to a considerable extent.

I have caused many of those subjects to be accurately copied, and engraved by hands eminent in their respective lines. The greatest attention has been paid by the ingenious artist, Mr. Haughton of the Royal Academy, taking the portraits of the images and the drawings of the pictures for my plates; which may be relied on as faithful representations of the original subjects.

My work has exceeded in bulk, although I have well filled both page and plate (for the plates contain nearly two thousand mythological figures, attributes, and subjects). Being unable to read the sacred books of the Brahmins, as Mr. Wilkins, Mr. Colebrooke, Mr. Wilford and others are, and as Sir William Jones (alas!) was, I have freely availed myself of the labours of these learned gentlemen.

To Mr. Wilkins, whose kindness has been so promptly extended to me on every occasion, mythological and miscellaneous, I must return thanks in a more pointed manner; and should do it more particularly, were it not that the pride, which I cannot conceal, of the countenance and friendship of a man of such rare talents and virtues, might wear the semblance of a display of vanity and egotism.

There can, I think, be but little doubt of the mythological legends of the Hindus being the source whence have been derived the fables and deities of Greece and Italy, and other heathen people of the West, a relationship highly interesting, it is not my purpose to enter into any disquisitions in proof of such origin, I have, indeed, avoided the subject. I have casually noticed some coincidences; but I leave to learned writers any general comparison of such deities throughout their manifold agreements in origin, name, character, attributes, and other points of presumable identity.

Contents

Nataraja, The Dancer Siva

1

Brahman and Three Gods: Brahma, Vishnu, Siva

The religious doctrines of the Hindus may be divided, like those of most other people whose scriptures are in a hidden tongue, into exoteric and esoteric; the first is preached to the masses, the second known only to a select number; and while the Brahmins are admitted to possess a considerable portion of unadulterated physical and moral truths, the exoteric religion of the Hindus, in general, consists of idolatry.

The doctrines thus divided, may be styled religion and mythology; the latter is perhaps the invention rather of poets than of priests; but being so well adopted to their purpose, the priests have artfully applied it to rivet the mental chains that, when the scriptures are concealed, they seldom fail to assist in forging for mankind.

Strictly speaking, the religion of the Hindus is monotheism. They worship God in unity, and express their conceptions of the Divine Being and his attributes in the most awful and sublime terms. God, thus

adored, is called Brahman: the One Eternal Mind, the self-existing, incomprehensible Spirit.

The Triad

After this we enter a field of allegory, so wide and so diversified, and at first sight so apparently confused and contradictory, that much ingenious research was found necessary, among its early cultivators, to reduce it to any regular arrangement; and much remains still to be done, before the inquirer can be repaid by the development of those truths that are unquestionably lured in the amazing mass of mythology.

The will of God, that the world should exist and continue, is personified; and his creative and preservative powers appear in Brahma and Vishnu, while Siva is the emblem of his destructive energy; not, however, of absolute annihilation, but rather of reproduction in another form.

In mythology, therefore, **this triad of persons represent the almighty powers of creation, preservation, and destruction.** In metaphysics Brahma is matter, Vishnu spirit and Siva time; or, in natural philosophy, earth, water, and fire.

Once deviating from rational devotion, the ardent mind of man knows no bounds: these three persons are hence fabled to have wives, the executors of the divine will, the energies of their respective lords. The fables arising from sexual allegories can scarcely fail of degenerating into indelicacy although we may admit that many historical and scientific truths lie concealed in their moral.

The rage for personification is unbounded: the sun, moon, and all the heavenly hosts; fire, air, and all natural phenomena; all nature indeed is animated passions and emotions of human beings, their vices and virtues are transformed into persons, and act appropriate parts in the turbulent history of man.

The preservative and regenerative powers, being in constant action, are feigned to have descended on earth innumerable times, in diverse places, for the instruction and benefit, including the profitable punishment, of mankind. The wives and children these powers have also, like their lords and parents, descended and assumed an infinite variety of forms on earth for similar purposes. **The history of these endless incarnations affords ample scope for the imagination; and they are worked up by the poets with wonderful fertility of genius and pomp of language into a variety of sublime descriptions,** interspersed with theological and moral texts, that at length were received as inspired productions, and have become the standard of divine truth.

Of Brahma, the deity's creative energy, less appears to have been said and sung than comparatively of the other coequal members of the triad; he has, like them, his consort and offspring, and has had terrestrial incarnations;

but the work of creation being past, Brahma, its represented power, is no longer especially adored in temples dedicated exclusively to him; associated with the other deities, offerings are gratefully made, and invocations piously addressed to the primary person; but as his portion of divine activity does not operate on the present hopes and fears of enthusiastic, or trembling suppliants, the exclusive and special adoration of Brahma is less ardent than hope or fear; in time it becomes overpowered by their superior potency, and its object is in a manner forgotten.

But a Hindu, spurning at sobriety of narration, cannot plainly state any historical or philosophical fact; it must have a fabulous and mythological origin, progress and termination; hence the three sects, who separately worshipped the coequal, coeternal powers, have, by a series of poetical persecution and warfare, in which the followers of Brahma were discomfited, his temples overthrown, and his worship abolished, been reduced to two; and the sects of Vaishnava and Saiva now comprise all the individuals of that very numerous race, distinguished by the appellation of Hindus.

These two sects, or grand divisions, are variously subdivided, as will be unfolded in the course of our work; but the whole, with the exception of the philosophic few, are influenced by a superstitious and idolatrous polytheism. The ignorant address themselves to idols fashioned by the hand of man, the sage worships God in spirit.

Of that infinite, incomprehensible, self-existent Spirit, no representation is made: to his direct and immediate honour no temples rise; nor dare a Hindu address to him the effusions of his soul otherwise than by the mediation of a personified attribute, or through the intervention of a priest; who will teach him that gifts, prostration, and sacrifice are good because they are pleasing to the gods; not, as an unsophisticated heart must feel, that piety and benevolence are pleasing to God because they are good.

But, **although the Hindus are taught to address their vows to idols and saints, these are still but types and personifications of the Deity, who is too awful to be contemplated, and too incomprehensible to be described;** still the ardour and enthusiasm of sectaries, when representing the object of their own exclusive adoration, dictate very awful and sublime effusions, exalting him into the throne of the Almighty, and arraying him in all the attributes of the Most High. It is, therefore, under the articles allotted to the description of persons and attributes, and sects and symbols, that our attention will be chiefly arrested and detained. As the Hindu erects no altars to Brahman, so we shall in this place make him but a brief offering of our consideration; in imitation of sectorial devotees, we shall dwell longer on the contemplation of created or imaginary beings, and haply aided by a ray of their philosophic light, look through nature up to nature's God.

"Of Him, whose glory is so great, there is no image," says the Veda. I can give no representation in the engraved portion of my work; nor shall I here detain the reader, but proceed to the consideration of the personified attributes of that invisible, incomprehensible Being, "which illumines all, delights all, whence all proceeded; that by which they live when born, and that to which all must return."

Brahma

Brahma is the personification of the creative power of the Deity, and although the name of the three most familiar perhaps to readers, is, in fact, not so often heard of in India as either of the other two great powers of preservation and destruction; or as of several other deities, or incarnations of deities, of all inferior description. Images are made of Brahma, and, placed in the temples of other gods, he is reverently propitiated by offerings and invocations; and he has had, like Vishnu and Siva, also incarnations, or avataras, but he has no temples, as many other deities have, or rites, exclusively dedicated to him.

The act of creation is past; the creative power of the Deity has no immediate interference in the continuance or cessation of material existence, or, in other words, with

Brahma, the Creator

the preservation or destruction of the universe. At a stated time the creative power will again be called into action, as will be noticed when we speak of the period Kalpa, till when, the powers of preservation and destruction only excite the hopes and fears of the devotee.

But as, according to the generally received theory, destruction—as we must occasionally, although in view to such theory, rather unphilosophically, term the effects of the destroying power—is only reproduction in another form; and as creation is a modification of a pre-existing formation of matter, the creative, as well as the destructive power, is thus admitted to be also, although less evidently, in constant action. Such action is, however, inevitable in its results, and the principle or power exciting it is less ardently, and less conspicuously, invoked and propitiated, than its dreaded destructive and contingent precursor; although their reciprocal action and reaction have caused a sort of unity of character; and Brahma and Siva are sometimes found almost identified with each other; oftener, however, in direct opposition and hostility. Brahma creates, Siva destroys; but to destroy is to create in another form; Siva and Brahma hence coalesce.

In mythology, therefore, **Brahma is the first of the three great personified attributes of Brahman or the Supreme Being.** He is called first of the gods; framer of the universe; guardian of the world; under the latter character, agreeing with Vishnu. In physics, he is the personification of matter generally, from him all things are created, and in him pre-existed the universe; comprehending all material forms, which he at once called into creation, or arranged existence, as they are now seen; although perpetually changing their appearances by the operation of the reproductive power. As the oak exists in the acorn, or rather, as the Hindu would express it, as the fruit is in the seed, awaiting development and expansion, so all material forms existed in Brahma, and their germs were at once produced by him.

From his mouth, arm, thigh, and foot, proceeded severally the priest, the warrior, the trader, and the labourer; these by successive reproduction people the earth; the sun sprung from his eye, and the moon from his mind.

Brahma is usually represented with four faces, said to represent the four quarters of his own work; and said, sometimes, to refer to a supposed number of elements of which he composed it; and to the sacred Vedas, one of which issued from each mouth. There are legends of his having formerly had five heads, one having been cut off by Siva, who is himself sometimes five-headed.

Red is the colour supposed to be peculiar to the creative power: we often see pictures of Brahma of that colour; which also represents fire, and its type the Sun; it is likewise the colour of the earth or matter, which Brahma also is; Brahma is, therefore, the earth; so we shall, by and by, find is Vishnu—Brahma is fire, so is Siva, and all three are the Sun; and the Sun is a symbol of Brahma, the Eternal One. Fire is an emblem of the all-changing, that is Time; Siva generally, and Brahma occasionally, correspond with Time. I thus early notice this agreement, or contradiction, or whatever it be, as I shall have occasion frequently, in the course of my humble work, to bring it to the reader's recollection, that **most, if not all, of the gods of the Hindu Pantheon, will, on close investigation, resolve themselves into the three powers, and those powers into one Deity, Brahman, typified by the Sun.**

Keeping this in view we may perhaps account for the disagreement discernible in the different accounts relating to the theogony of the Hindus. They are, as we shall have occasion often to notice, divided into sects, each sect worshipping some individual deity, or two or more conjoined; such individual deity is gifted by its votary with all the attributes of the Most High, and is made the source whence emanate all other gods. Although there is, I believe, no sect named after Brahma, denoting him to be the exclusive object of their adoration, yet by some legends he is described as the Almighty; and even his spouse, or Sakti, Saraswati, as we shall find when we come to notice her, is described as all-productive, all-powerful, and all-wise.

Thus, if a Vaishnava speaks or writes of Vishnu, he is actually described as the Deity:

if one of the adored incarnations, or avataras of Vishnu, (Krishna, or Rama, for instance) he is likewise omnipotent and omniscient—he is Vishnu. The same of Siva, when described by one of his own sect, he is the very God of every God; this may be extended even to inferior gods and goddesses. A poet, meaning to describe their energy, calls them omnipotent; their wisdom, they are omniscient; their activity, they are omnipresent; hence arises a confusion that embarrasses the inquirer at every step; "gods meet with gods, and jostle in the dark;" and being ultimately resolvable into one, as that one is approached, the clashing seems more and more frequent.

Mr. Colebrooke, in a paper has the following, applicable to this topic:

"The deities invoked appear, on a cursory inspection of the Veda, to be as various as the authors of the prayers addressed to them; but, according to the most ancient annotations on the Indian scripture, those numerous names of persons and things are all resolvable into different titles of three deities, and ultimately of one God. The *Nighantu*, or glossary of the Vedas, concludes with three lists of names of deities: the first comprising such as are deemed synonymous with fire; the second, with air; and the third, with the sun. In the last part of the *Nirukta*, which entirely relates to deities, it is twice asserted that there are but three gods: *'Tisra eva devatah.'* The further inference, that these intend but one deity, is supported by many passages in the Veda, and is very clearly and concisely stated in the beginning of the index to the Rig Veda, on the authority of the *Nirukta*, and of the Veda itself.

"The deities are only three, whose places are the earth, the intermediate region, and heaven; fire, air, and the sun. They are pronounced to be the deities of the mysterious names severally; and Prajapati, the lord of creatures, is the deity of them collectively, The syllable Om intends every deity: it appertains to Brahma the vast one; to God; to Adhyatma, the superintending soul. Other deities, belonging to these several regions, are portions of the three gods; for they are variously named and described on account of their different operations; but in fact there is only One Deity, the Great Soul, Mahanatma. He is called the Sun; for he is the soul of all beings; and that is declared by the sage: 'The Sun is the soul of *jagat*, what moves, and of *tatnush*, that which is fixed.' Other deities are portions of him; and that is expressly declared by the sage: 'The wise call fire Indra, Mitra and Varuna,' etc."

"This passage, taken from different parts of the Veda, shows," says Mr. Colebrooke, "what is also deducible from other texts of the Indian scriptures, that the ancient Hindu religion, as founded on the Indian scriptures, recognises but one God; yet not sufficiently discriminating the creature from the Creator." (*On the Vedas*. Asiatic Researches. Vol. VIII)

The names of Brahma are not so numerous as those of his great coadjutors. Vishnu and Siva are said to have a thousand each. He is sometimes called Kamalayoni. Kamal is the lotus, Yoni the *pudendum muliebre,* or the creative power, the mystical matrix, into which is inserted the equally mysterious Linga of Siva. Brahma having, by a generally received system, founded on the doctrines of the Vaishnava, sprang on a lotus from the navel of Vishnu, to "bid all worlds exist," has hence, and perhaps in other points, relation to the lotus; but it is a more immediate attribute of Vishnu, being the prime of aquatic vegetables; and he, a personification of water. His consort, Lakshmi, in one character, sprang from the sea; and the lotus, being also the emblem of female beauty, is peculiarly sacred to her; and she is called Kamala, or lotus-like.

All the principal, and several of the secondary deities, or incarnations of the principal, have wives assigned to them, who are called Sakti; and, except in sex, exactly represent their respective lords, being their energy, or active power—the executors of their divine will. The Sakti of Brahma is Saraswati, the goddess of harmony and the arts.

Many deities have, as well as wives, vehicles, or *vahanas,* allotted to them; that of Brahma, and of his Sakti, is the swan, or goose, called Hansa; but he is not so frequently seen mounted on it; as other deities are on theirs.

In the picture given here he is seen in his usual form, with four faces, and four arms, having in his hands, what his descendants, the Brahmins, are supposed to have often in theirs, a portion of the Veda, or scripture; a spoon, used in the performance of sacred ceremonies, for lustral water; a rosary for assisting abstraction, in contemplating the attributes of God, a bead being dropped at the mental recitation of each of his names, while the mind is intensely fixed on the idea that the name, which is significant of some attribute, excites; and, fourthly, a vessel to contain water for ablution, a preliminary essential to prayer.

Vishnu

If the term 'orthodox' can, in strictness, be applied to any sect of Hindus, it appears most appropriate to that of the Vaishnavas, or general worshippers of Vishnu. They admit the independent existence of the other personified attributes, but claim a superiority for that of preservation. Nothing, they say, can be actually destroyed; the operation of the destructive power varies the form of matter; but it is only changed, not annihilated; reproduced, not destroyed; hence they infer the paramount power of preservation.

Vishnu is the second person of the Hindu triad; he is a personification of the preserving power, and has, on the whole, no doubt, a greater number of adorers than any other deity or attribute.

He is a personification of the Sun, or, conversely, the Sun is a type of him; this

Vishnu, the Preserver

character, as well as that of Time, he shares with Brahma and Siva—in Hindu mythology everything is, indeed, the Sun. Vishnu is sometimes the earth—he is water, or the humid principle generally; hence he is air, which the Hindus know to be a form of humidity. He is also space, and his colour is blue, supposed to be its apparent tint.

Mounted on an eagle, or rather an animal composed of the eagle and the man, named Garuda, Vishnu is seen cleaving his own element, and soaring to the skies. This marks the aerial levity of his character, as the sluggish goose is emblematic of gravity. His Sakti or consort, is Lakshmi.

The following verses are a translation from the *Bhagavat* by Sir William Jones; they are supposed to have been pronounced by the Supreme Being Brahma. The Bhagavat, being the work of a Vaishnava, of course speaks of Vishnu as that Being, or rather of Krishna, identified by his sectaries with the preserving power.

"Even I was at first, not any other thing, that which exists unperceived, supreme, afterwards, I am that which is; and he who must remain, am I.

"Except the First Cause, whatever may appear, and may not appear in the mind, know that to be the mind's Maya, or Delusion, as light, as darkness.

"As the great elements are in various beings, yet not entering (that is, pervading, not destroying), thus am I in them, yet not in them.

"Even thus far may inquiry be made by him who seeks to know the principle of mind, in union and separation, which must be everywhere always."

The following legends will introduce us to the character of Vishnu, and other points connected with him.

It is related in the *Skanda Purana* that, when the whole earth was covered with water, and Vishnu lay extended asleep on the bosom of Devi, a lotus arose from his navel, and its ascending flower soon reached the surface of the flood; that Brahma sprang from that flower, and, looking round without seeing a creature on the boundless expanse, imagined himself to be the first born, and entitled to rank above future beings; yet, resolved to investigate the deep, and to ascertain whether any being existed in it who could controvert his claim to pre-eminence, he glided, therefore, down the stalk of the lotus, and finding Vishnu asleep, asked loudly who he was?

'I am the first born,' answered Vishnu; and when Brahma denied his primogeniture, they had an obstinate battle, till Mahadeva pressed between them in great wrath, saying, 'It is I who am truly the first born; but I will resign my pretensions to either of you, who shall be able to reach and behold the summit of my head, or the soles of my feet.'

Brahma instantly ascended; but having fatigued himself to no purpose in the regions of immensity, yet loth to abandon his claim,;

returned to Mahadeva, declaring that he had attained and seen the crown of his head, and called as his witness the first born cow. For this union of pride and falsehood, the angry god ordained, that no sacred rites should be performed to Brahma, and that the mouth of the cow should be defiled, and a cause of defilement, as it is declared to be in the oldest Indian laws.

When Vishnu returned, he acknowledged that he had not been able to see the feet of Mahadeva, who then told him that he was the first born among the gods, and should be raised above all. It was after this, that Mahadeva cut off the fifth head of Brahma, whose pride occasioned his loss of power and influence in the countries bordering on the river Kali.

Another legend makes Siva the offspring of Vishnu.

It is said, in the *Vaishnavagama*, that Krodhasura was a demon with the face of a boar, who, nevertheless, was continually reading the Veda, and performing such acts of devotion that Vishnu appeared to him on the banks of the Brahmaputra, promising to grant any boon that he could ask. Krodhasura requested that no creature then existing in the three worlds might have power to deprive him of life, and Vishnu complied with his request; but the demon became so insolent, that the Devatas, whom he oppressed, were obliged to conceal themselves, and he assumed the dominion of the world. Vishnu was then sitting on the bank of the Kali, greatly disquieted by the malignant ingratitude of the demon; and, his wrath being kindled, a shape, which never before had existed, sprang from his eyes. It was Mahadeva in his destructive character, who dispelled in a moment the anxiety of Vishnu: whence he acquired the surname of Chintahara.

Vishnu and Siva are each said to have a thousand names; and as they are in most instances significant compound Sanskrit words, there are legends in the Puranas, and other books, accounting for the origin and application of such names.

The thousand names of Vishnu and Siva are strung together in verse, and are repeated on certain occasions by Brahmins, as a sort of litany, accompanied sometimes with the rosary. As each name is mentally recited, with the attention abstractedly fixed on the attribute, or character, that such name excites the idea of, a bead is dropped through the finger and thumb; such operation is supposed to assist and promote abstraction, an attainment that enthusiastic Hindus think exceedingly efficacious.

The use of rosaries is adopted in India, and perhaps in other countries of the east, Persia, for instance, by Mahomedans. With the Mahomedans the rosary seems to answer the same purpose as with the Hindus; a bead is dropped through the finger and thumb at the contemplation or repetition of certain names and attributes of God, who in the "copious rhetoric of Arabia" has as many appellations nearly as in Sanskrit.

Considering Vishnu as Time, he corresponds with the Horus of Egypt. There are legends of his sleeping, and turning on his side, evidently alluding to the Sun at the solstices; also the phenomenon of the overflow and receding of the Ganges. On the 11th day (sometimes on the 14th, which is the day of the full moon), of the bright half of the lunar month Kartika, Vishnu is fabled to rise from his slumber of four months. A festival is held in honour of this day, and at an auspicious moment, astrologically determined, the Deity is awakened by this incantation:

"The clouds are dispersed, the full moon will appear in perfect brightness, and I come in hope of acquiring purity, to offer the fresh flowers of the season; awake from thy long slumber; awake! Lord of all worlds!"

Another festival occurs on the 11th of the bright half of the month Ashadha, when commences, with the summer solstice, the night of the Gods; and Vishnu reposes for four months on the serpent Sesha. Nine days afterwards, the fifth after the full moon, is a festival in honour of "Devi, the goddess of nature, surnamed Manasa; who, while Vishnu and all the gods were sleeping, sat in the shape of a serpent on a branch of Snuhi (Euphorbia) to preserve mankind from the venom of snakes."—We may here notice, although not immediately in the most appropriate place, that snakes and serpents have a conspicuous niche in the Hindu Pantheon. The fifth day of the bright half of the month Sravana, which day is called Nagapanchami, is sacred to the demigods in the form of serpents, who are enumerated in the *Padma* and *Garuda Puranas*. Doors of houses are smeared with cow dung and Nimba leaves, as a preservative from poisonous reptiles.

Both in the *Padma* and *Garuda Puranas*, we find the serpent Kaliya, whom Krishna slew in his childhood, among the deities worshipped on this day.

When we speak of the symbolical marks of the Hindus, we shall find the triangle, with the apex downwards, to be the appropriate symbol of Vishnu, considered as the principle of humidity. To descend is the property of water, and it naturally assumes that figure. Nor is the triangle, with the apex pointing upwards, a less appropriate symbol of Siva, as Fire; it being the unvaried form of the igneous element, whose property is ascension.

The paradise, or celestial abode of Vishnu, is called Vaikuntha, where he enjoys beatitude in the elysium of Lakshmi's lap.

Images and pictures of Vishnu, either representing him in his person, or in any of his Avataras, or incarnations, may be generally distinguished from those of other deities by a shell, Shankh, and a sort of wheel, or discus, called Chakra. The Shankh is the large buccinum, sometimes seen beautifully coloured like a pheasant's breast. The Chakra is a missile weapon, very like our quoit, having a hole in its centre, on which it is twirled by the forefinger, and thrown at the destined object.

It has a sharp edge, and irresistible fire flames from its periphery when whirled by Vishnu. Two other attributes appertain generally to Vishnu: these are the Gada and Padma; the former a mace or club, the latter a lotus. But these last are oftener seen in the hands of his Avataras, than in those of Vishnu himself; and of the four attributes, the Shankh is, I think, that which, on the whole, most distinguishes Vishnu.

The perpendicular lines on the forehead of a devotee, are said to be the distinction of the Vaishnavas from the Saivas, the latter having them horizontal.

Vishnu has had his Avataras, or terrestrial incarnations. It is related in the Puranas, that in Vishnu's seventh grand Avatara, of Rama Chandra, Sesha was born in a human shape as his half brother, son of Dasaratha, Raja of Ayodhya, by his second wife, Sumitra, and named Lakshmana; Rama himself being born at the same time of the Raja's first wife, Kausalya.

In the Avatara of Krishna, Sesha was Balarama, Krishna's elder brother by the same parents, Vasudeva and Devaki, the latter sister of Kansa.

We cannot better close our general account of the preserving member of the Hindu triad, than with an animated passage from the conclusion of the *Gita Govinda,* a pastoral mythological dramatic poem in Sanskrit glorifying Vishnu, by Jayadeva:

"Whatever is delightful in the modes of music; whatever is divine in meditations on Vishnu; whatever is exquisite in the sweet art of love; whatever is graceful in the fine strains of poetry, all that let the happy and wise learn from the songs of Jayadeva, whose soul is united to the foot of Narayana. May that Hari be your support, who expanded himself into an infinity of bright forms, when, eager to gaze with myriads of eyes on the daughter of the ocean, he displayed his great character of the all-pervading Deity, by the multiplied reflections of his divine person in the numberless gems on the many heads of the king of serpents whom he chose for his couch; that Hari, who, removing the lucid veil from the bosom of Padma, and fixing his eyes on the delicious buds that grew on it, diverted her attention, by declaring that when she had chosen him as her bridegroom, near the sea

of milk, the disappointed husband of Parvati drank in despair the venom which dyed his neck azure."

Siva

Siva is generally **ranked as the third power or attribute of the Deity: he personifies destruction, or rather reproduction;** for the most popular system of Hindu philosophy excludes, while time shall exist, the idea of absolute annihilation: to destroy is, therefore, but to change, or recreate, or reproduce. And here we at once see how easy it is to confound the characters aud powers of Siva and Brahma, and to imagine the deity of destruction to preside also over generation.

In the obvious arrangement of the three grand powers of the Eternal One, creation and preservation precede destruction; and this is the relative philosophical and mythological rank of the triad, but not always their theological or sectarial station. For as the Vaishnavas exalt Vishnu, so the Saivas exalt Siva to the place, and describe him with the power of the Deity, or Brahman as all things must, at the end of Time, suffer destruction; so the personification of that power must be considered as ultimately paramount, although, anterior to that inconceivable period, the preserving member of the Trinity may have apparent predominancy.

He is Time, the Sun; he is Fire, the destroyer, the generator. His consort, Bhavani, is the symbol of created nature, and in that

Siva, the Destroyer—with Parvati on Mount Kailas

character named Prakriti. As the deity presiding over generation, his type is the Linga. As the God of Justice, which character he shares with Yama and other deities, he rides a bull, the symbol of divine justice. He holds, as his commonest attribute, a trident, called Trisula; in this, and in some other points, resembling our Neptune; his consort also has a relationship to water, although Vishnu be generally the deity presiding over humidity. His colour, as well as that of his bull, is white; I know not why, unless it refers to the unsullied purity of justice; his hair is of a light or reddish colour. He is sometimes seen with two hands, at others with four, eight, or ten, and with five faces. He has a third eye in his forehead, pointing up and down: this distinction is, I think, peculiar to him, and his children and Avataras. As emblems of immortality, serpents are a common ornament with many deities; but Mahadeva seems most abundantly bedecked with them: bound in his hair, round his neck, wrists, waist, arms, and legs, as well as for rings, snakes are his constant attendants. A crescent on his forehead, or in his hair, is common in pictures and images of Mahesa, or Siva.

Serpents, emblems of eternity, form his ear-rings, called Nag Kundala; his pendent collar of human heads Mundmala, marks his character of destruction, or Time; and his frontal crescent points at its most obvious measurement, by the phases of the moon.

These are among the attributes that generally distinguish Mahadeva.

In a statue this deity has been represented with a warlike weapon (Gada, or Parashu) and an antelope in his superior hands; the former, as with many other deities, denoting vengeance, and almost all of them seem occasionally to act as its ministers; the latter, called Mriga, an attribute of the god Chandra, the Moon; called also Sasin, a name for the antelope, given likewise to Chandra. Siva's loins are wrapped in a tiger's skin, an article that will be frequently seen in the plates of this deity; and the river goddess Ganga. beams benignly from his Mukut, or headpiece.

This bountiful goddess Ganga is a heroine frequently alluded to in the mythological and historical legends of the Hindus. The Hindu poets, in their rage for personification, have not of course forgotten those grand natural objects, rivers: these prime gifts of beneficent nature are deified. The Ganga, Yamuna, Saraswati, Brahmaputra, Krishna, Kaveri and others, enjoy their apotheosis; and there are extant numerous allegorical poems descriptive of their birth, loves, etc.

Sir William Jones, in the true spirit of a Hindu bard, has addressed a hymn to the goddess Ganga, who is fabled to be the offspring of Mahadeva, and he sings her birth, wanderings, and nuptials, with Brahma's son, the Brahmaputra.

"Is that the King of Dread,
With ashy musing face;
From whose moon-silver'd locks Ganga springs?"

The pictures offered for sale in India are generally coloured; and Siva, the King of Dread, whose characteristic colour is white, is often painted as if rubbed over with ashes, like anchorites or penitents, with a blue throat. In those pictures we see the river Ganga falling from his head; and sometimes, as she afterwards issues, from a cow's mouth. It is said that high up towards its source, the river passes through a narrow rocky passage, that pilgrims who visit the sacred cleft, imagine it resembles a cow's mouth. This spot is hence called Gomukh and is a pilgrimage of great resort.

The following stanza, from Sir William Jones; spirited hymn to Ganga will introduce and illustrate, in a happier manner, some of the engraved subjects:

"Above the stretch of mortal ken,
On bless'd Kailasa's top where every stem
Glow'd with a vegetable gem,
Mahesh sat, the dread and joy of men,
While Parvati, to gain a boon,
Fix'd on hill locks a beamy moon,
And hid his frontal eye, in jocund play,
With reluctant sweet delay,
All nature straight was lock'd in dim eclipse.
Till Brahman pure, with hallow'd lips
And warbled prayers, restored the day,

When Ganga from his brow, by heavenly fingers prest,
Sprang radiant, and descending, grac'd the caverns of the West."

Ganga, Chandra, and Seshnaga, the prince of serpents, are generally seen on Siva's head as his commonest ornaments; and poets perpetually advert to him in compound epithets, allusive to those distinguishing attributes.

But the Vaishnavas, unwilling to attribute so great a boon exclusively to another deity, assert, that the blessed and blessing river flowed originally out of Vaikuntha, from the foot of Vishnu, and, descending upon Kailasa, fell on the head of Siva; who, when he received the divine stream from on high, shook some drops from his hair, which are called Bindu, and form a great lake far to the north of Hindustan, called Bindu Sarovara.

Both the Vaishnavas and Saivas are naturally anxious to attribute to the deity of their exclusive adoration, as well all power, might, and dominion, the origin of acts of favour and beneficence. Both sects partake of the bountiful blessings of the Ganges, and each is desirous of tracing its source to the head or foot of its own deity.

But, although the Vaishnavas far outnumber the adherents of Siva, it appears to me that the latter god has generally the reputation of having produced this river. I have many pictures, a dozen or more, where it flows from Siva's hair, but not one in which it proceeds from Vishnu's foot.

The Ganga is also called Dasahara, or ten-removing; meaning to remove ten sins. Bathing in her waters, on the day named in the following couplet, effaces ten sins, how heinous-soever, committed in ten previous births.

"On the tenth of Jaishtha. in the bright half of the month; on the day of Mangala, son of the earth, when the moon was in Hasta, this daughter of Jahnu burst from the rocks, and flowed over the land inhabited by mortals.

"On this lunar day, therefore, she washes off ten sins, and gives a hundred times more felicity than could be attained by myriads of Aswamedhas, or sacrifices of a horse."

Another legend states, that the anniversary of the first day of the Satyayug is sacred, on account of Ganga having thereon flowed from the foot of Vishnu down upon the Himalaya, where she was received on the head of Siva, and was afterwards led to the ocean by King Bhagiratha. Hence adoration is now paid to Ganga, Himalaya, Sankara and his mountain Kailash; nor must Bhagiratha be neglected

Those who are not so happy as to live near the holy river, make pilgrimages for the purpose of benefiting by its sin-expelling water; if unable to perform the pilgrimage in person, there is considerable efficacy in doing it by proxy, paying the expenses of an idler man;

who, in return, frequently brings his principal a jar of the precious fluid, to be used in the time of death and need. Many persons are constantly employed In bringing Ganga's water to distant parts. Temples of celebrity, however remote, those of Rameswara and Jejury for instance, are said to use it daily for the ablution of the idol; and in every city it may be purchased from persons who carry it about in two vases, slung at the ends of a bamboo carried across the shoulders: these are carefully covered, and of course preserved with veneration.

One of the holiest spots of the Ganga is where it joins the Yamuna near Allahabad. The Saraswati is supposed to join them underground, whence the junction is called Triveni, or the three-plaited locks; pilgrims here begin the ceremonies afterwards completed at Gaya. The confluence of rivers is a spot peculiarly dear to Hindus; and this, more specially, of the Ganga and Yamuna, is so highly esteemed, that a person dying there is certain of immediate *moksha,* or beatitude, without risk of further transmigration.

Paterson, in *Asiatic Researches,* Vol. VIII, writes:

"To Siva is given three eyes, probably to denote his view of the three divisions of Time: the past, the present, and the future. A crescent on his forehead portrays the measure of time by the phases of the moon; a serpent forms a necklace to denote the measure of time by years; a second necklace, formed of human skulls, marks the lapse and revolution of ages and the extinction and succession of the generations of mankind. He holds a trident, to show that the three great attributes are in him assembled and united; in another hand is a kind of rattle, called Damaru."

In the hieroglyphic of Maha Pralaya, or grand consummation of all things, when Time itself shall be no more, he is represented as trodden under foot by Mahakala, or Eternity.

Mahakala, as represented in the caverns of Elephanta, has eight arms. In one he holds a human figure; in another a sword, or sacrificial axe; in third he holds a basin of blood, and with a fourth be rings over it the sacrificial bell. Two other arms are broken off; with the two remaining he is drawing behind him a veil, which extinguishes the Sun, and involves the whole universe in one undistinguished ruin. One of the titles of this tremendous deity is Bhairava, the terrific; but his principal designation is Kalagni Rudra.

Having been in the Elephanta Caves, and when there made some memoranda, I will in this place extract from them what relates to the subject of Mahakala. The compartment containing the group, of which Siva in this character makes the principal figure, is on the right of the entrance, facing a compartment of like size, containing what, in another part of this work, I have supposed to be a marriage ceremony. Between the two compartments, but advanced into the body of the cave so as not to be interposed, is a room, twenty-two feet square, with a door in each face, and on each side of the doors a gigantic male figure, in stature sixteen feet, highly ornamented; this room contains a monstrous Linga. Premising this, I proceed to extract from my notes an account of the compartment containing the figure in question.

It is of Siva Vindex, fourteen feet high, but his lower extremities broken off; his attention is, from his attitude, turned to his left; his aspect is terrific, indicating the immediate execution of some avenging act; he has eight arms; the superior right and left stretched up, and either supporting a cloth or curtain, or pulling it over the terrible event he threatens; the fingers grasp the cloth; the left upstretched arm finely executed; the right broken at the elbow; his next right hand is broken off at the wrist; the corresponding left holds a bell in good preservation, over a cup in the palm of the next, having a serpent twining round near the elbow. A third right panel grasps a long straight sword, uplifted, perfect; the two inferior hands, right and left, are broken off above the elbow; they were in bolder relief, and the left appears to have supported, or to have grasped, the leg of a kneeling figure, the trunk of which only remains, its legs, arms, and head, being broken off; this kneeling figure may have been between five and six feet in height; its back is toward the threatener, and leaning so in his direction as to drop its blood, if spilled, into the cup before noticed.

The head of the principal figure has a highly ornamented cap reminding one of the mitre-shaped caps worn some years ago by our grenadiers; a skull and serpent are among its frontal ornaments. It has also a pendent necklace, and a long chaplet, if I may so call it, composed of human heads, of which on it two or three are plainly discernible, flowing over the left shoulder to the right thigh, where it is broken off; the holy thread, and a broader belt, run in nearly a like direction; on all the wrists are bracelets; and above the elbows of three of the arms are *bazubands*. No figures remain in any preservation to the right of the principal, or under him. On the left, near the supposed victim, are two bearded faces expressive of pity: a compassionate female is just above them, leaning forward over the victim; she holds her scarf in her hands, and is an elegant person; below the bearded men are two or three females with pitying aspects; the same emotion, intermingled with terror, is evident in every face of this compartment, whose features can be traced.

Over the subjects just described is a row of males and females of rather diminutive size; in the middle of the row, nearly over the head of Siva, is a thing like a mitre, with a crosier cut deep in it, and surmounted with a cross; but the limbs of the cross not exactly at right angles; two aged and emaciated males are on the right—the spectator's right—of the mitre holding up their hands, betokening pity and pain; on the other side of the mitre are two similar figures; in front of each pair is a prostrate distressed male child, their heads near the mitre; beyond the last mentioned pair, on the spectator's left, are a male and female in great anxiety and distress, holding scarfs in their hands.

The subject, supposed to be like a mitre, crosier, and cross, appears also, in a compartment before described, as containing characters in the background; fancy may, perhaps, have had some share in making this resemblance; but it is really curious, and I think striking, although I believe, hitherto, not remarked.

Siva is also called Sri Virupaksha, or the three-eyed god. This name of Sri Virupaksha is, however, differently translated by different Sanskrit scholars. The earliest renders it as above; another, "with a disagreeable countenance"; a third, "the auspicious deity with uneven eyes"; and as the title is also given to an inferior deity, who is not fabled to have three eyes, Nirut, I am disposed to think the latter interpretations are to be preferred.

A poet, in his extravagant praises of a king, gives the following hyperbolical reason for Mahadeva's third eye, and for the attributes that distinguish other deities:

"The gods had apprehensions in the beginning of time that the glory of so great a monarch would rapidly diffuse one vast blaze over the universe, and leave them without marks of distinction; thence it was that Purari

assumed a third eye in his forehead, Padmaksha four arms, Atmabhu four faces; that Kali holds in her hands a cemeter, Rama a lotus, and Vani a lyre."

In this adulation the poet seemed desirous also to show his learning, for it is not common to hear Mahadeva denominated as Purari. I recollect but one instance in which Kama, the god of love, is called foe or Purari, in allusion to his attempt of exciting an amorous passion in the bosom of the angry deity.

Visweshwara, an epithet derived I apprehend from Viswa, all, and Iswara, Lord, is the name by which Siva is invoked at a beautiful and famous temple of that name in Kashi, or Benares; and it is said in the Puranas that "the Vedas and Sastras all testify that Visweshwara is the first of Devas, Kashi the first of cities, Ganga the first of rivers, and charity the first of virtues."

Mahadeva's vehicle, or Nandi, is a white bull, on which he is frequently seen riding. In his temples it is represented, sometimes of vast dimensions. It is very commonly met with in brass, etc., with and without the other symbols of Siva. It is understood to be a personification of divine justice, which moves or conveys the avenging power of the deity to the derserved punishment of mortals.

Ganesa and Kartika are the first and second sons of Mahadeva and Parvati. Of the sons of Mahadeva and Parvati, they are by far the most renowned. Bhairava and Virabhadra are two other reputed sons of Mahadeva.

• • •

2

Three Major Goddesses: Saraswati, Lakshmi, Parvati

Saraswati

In the *Asiatic Miscellany*, and in Sir William Jones' works will be found a spirited hymn, addressed to this goddess:

> *"Sweet grace of Brahma's bed.*
> *Whose sigh is music, and each tear a pearl"*

From the argument prefixed to it I extract the following passages:

"The Hindu goddesses are uniformly represented as the subordinate powers of their respective lords: thus Lakshmi, the consort of Vishnu the Preserver, is the goddess of abundance and prosperity; Bhavani, the wife of Mahadeva, is the genial power of fecundity; and **Saraswati, whose husband was the Creator Brahma, possesses the powers of imagination and invention, which may justly be termed creative. She is, therefore, adored as the patroness of the fine arts,** especially of music and rhetoric, as the inventress of the Sanskrit language, of the Devanagari characters, and of the sciences which writing perpetuates, so that her attributes correspond with those of Minerva Muslca, in Greece or Italy, who invented the flute, and presided over literature. The seven notes, an artful combination of which constitutes music, and variously affect the passions, are feigned to be her earliest production. And the greatest part of the hymn exhibits a correct delineation of the Ragmala, or Necklace of Musical Nodes, which may be considered as the most pleasing invention of the ancient Hindus, and the most beautiful union of painting with poetical mythology and the genuine theory of music."

The argument proceeds thus:

"A full discussion of so copious a subject would require a separate dissertation; but here it will be sufficient to say, that almost every allusion and every epithet in the poem, as well as the names, are selected from approved treatises.

"We thirst, Vakdevi, for thy balmy lore,
Drawn from that rubied cave
Where meek-eyed pilgrims hail the triple wave." (*Veda*)

The name Saraswati means flowing, applicable both to the river, and the goddess of eloquence. Vacha, Lepita, have meanings chiefly referrible to speech, or speaking. She is also called Vani, Brahmi or Brahmani, and by several other names.

The last line alludes to the celebrated place of pilgrimage, at the confluence of the

Saraswati, the Goddess of Creativity

Ganga and Yamuna, which the Saraswati, the third sacred river, is supposed to join underground.

The last watch of the night is peculiarly sacred to Saraswati.

"Let the housekeeper wake in the time sacred to Brahmi, the goddess of speech, that is in the last watch of the night; let him then reflect on virtue and virtuous emoluments, and on the whole meaning and very essence of the Veda." (Manu)

The fifth day of the month Magha is called Sri-panchami, on which Saraswati, or Sri, the goddess of arts and eloquence, is worshipped with offerings of perfumes, flowers, and dressed rice; even the implements of writing, and books, are treated with respect, and are not used on this holiday. The following meditation on this goddess will furnish a description of her person and attributes:

"May the goddess of speech enable us to attain all possible felicity: she who wears on her locks a young moon; who shines with exquisite lustre; whose body bends with the weight of her full breasts; who sits reclined on a white lotus; and from the crimson lotus of her hands pours radiance on the implements of writing, and on the books produced by her favour."

Saraswati is, among other deities, especially propitiated in the marriage ceremonies of the Brahmins; the following hymn is chanted in her honour:

"Charming Saraswati! swift as a mare, whom I celebrate in the face of this universe, protect this solemn rite. O thou! in whom the elements were produced, in whom this universe was framed, I will now sing that hymn" (the nuptial text) *"which constitutes the highest glory of women."*

Whatever deity a Hindu may have occasion to invoke, or rather whichever be the object of his adoration, whether god or goddess, superior or inferior, he will array his patron in the attributes of the Almighty himself. The ardent imagination of a poet knows no restraint; but we must recollect that a female deity is actually her Lord: Saraswati is the active energy or power of her consort Brahma—his Sakti; she is therefore endowed with his attribute of creation. And, in the preceding and following extracts, we see her, not unappropriately, invoked as the being in whom the elements were produced, in whom this universe was framed and also gifted with the peculiar power and attributes of other deities.

Near the close of the tenth book of the Rigveda, a hymn is spoken by each daughter of Ambhrina, in praise of herself as the supreme universal soul. Each signifies speech and she is the active power of Brahma, proceeding from him. The following is a literal version of this hymn, which is expounded by the commentator consistently with the theological doctrines of the Vedas:

"I range with the Rudras, with the Vasus, with the Adityas, and with the Visweshdevas. I uphold both the sun and the ocean (Mitra and Varuna), the firmament (Indra), and fire, and both the Aswins. I support the moon (Soma), destroyer of foes and the sun entitled Twashti, Pushan or Bhaga. I grant wealth to the honest votary who performs sacrifices, offers oblations, and satisfies the deities. Me, who am the queen, the conferrer of wealth, the possessor of knowledge, and first of such as merit worship, the gods render, universally, present everywhere, and provider of all beings. He who eats food through me, as he who sees, or who breathes, or who hears through me, yet knows me not, is lost; hear then the faith which I pronounce. Even I declare this self, who is worshipped by gods and men; I make strong whom I choose; I make him Brahma, holy and wise: for Rudra I bend the bow to slay the demon, foe of Brahma; for the people I make war on their foes; and I pervade heaven and earth. I bore the father on the head of this universal mind, and my origin is in the midst of the ocean; and therefore do I pervade all beings, and touch this heaven with my form. Originating all beings, I pass like the breeze; I am above this heaven, beyond this earth, and what is the great one, that am I."

In another page I have hinted my opinion, that more sects of Hindus—classes, I mean, who exclusively adore one deity, in person or through his Sakti—exist than we are at present aware of; at any rate, if they do not now exist, such passages as that last quoted almost prove that they have prevailed heretofore. No sect, or perhaps individual, now exclusively worships either Brahma or Saraswati; but, surely, the passage in question must have been penned or conceived by a sectarist of that deity.

In cases where a Hindu may have lied, or given false evidence, the sin is expiated by an easy oblation to the goddess of speech. A few texts from Manu will evince this:

"In some cases a giver of false evidence, from a pious motive, even though he knows the truth, shall not lose a seat in heaven; such evidence wise men call the speech of the gods.

"Whenever the death of a man, who had not been a grievous offender, either of the servile, the commercial, the military, or the sacerdotal class, would be occasioned by true evidence, from the known rigour of the king, even though the fall arose from inadvertence or error, falsehood may be spoken; it is even preferable to truth.

"Such witnesses must offer, as oblations to Saraswati, cakes of rice and milk addressed to the goddess of speech; and thus will they fully expiate the venal sin of benevolent falsehood."

Images of Saraswati are seldom seen; I have not one among my images, nor do I immediately recollect having ever seen one. Of pictures I have several; and some representations of her are given in our plates, of which I will now give some description.

She is usually drawn either two or four-handed; she is the immediate two-handed helpmate and associate of her husband Brahma; and has, of her own, no distinguishing attributes. In one picture she is four-handed, holding her Vina, a lotus, a cup, and a scroll.

In another she is also four-handed, playing on her Vina with two hands, the others empty; she is here riding a peacock, and not, as one would expect, a swan, the Vahan of her consort, which, indeed, I never saw her mounted on.

Saraswati in both pictures is dressed in a red Sari; in one a red, the other a green Choli; the peacock is blueish, with a green tail.

Lakshmi

Lakshmi is the consort of Vishnu, the Sakti, or active energy, of the personified preservative power. **She is considered as the goddess of riches,** and would be invoked for increase of wealth by a desiring Hindu rather than Kuvera, she might, therefore, be naturally considered as the appropriate consort of the deity of wealth.

The followers of Vishnu esteem Lakshmi as the mother of the world, and they call her Adi Maya; and such Vaishnavas as are Saktas, that is, adorers of the female energy or nature-active, worship her exclusively as the symbol of the Eternal Being. As Rambha, the sea-born

Lakshmi, the Goddess of Prosperity, with Vishnu

goddess of beauty, she sprang as one of the fourteen gems from the ocean, when churned by the good and evil beings for the Amrita, or immortal beverage.

In the 36th section of the *Ramayana*, describing the Kurmavatara, the production of Lakshmi is thus painted:

"The gods, the Asuras, and the Gandharvas, again agitating the sea, after a long time appeared the great goddess, inhabiting the lotus, clothed with superlative beauty, in the first bloom of youth, covered with ornaments, and bearing every auspicious sign: adorned with a crown, with bracelets on her arms, her jetty locks flowing in ringlets, and her body, which resembled burning gold, adorned with ornaments of pearl. This great goddess appeared with four arms, holding a lotus in her hand, her countenance incomparable in beauty. Thus was produced the goddess Padma, or Sri, adored by the whole universe, Padma by name. She took up her abode in the bosom of Padmanabha, even of Hari."

As the goddess of fortune, the epithet fickle is sometimes applied to Lakshmi, in contradistinction to Parvati, or Sati, who is called the constant, or faithful. In this fickle character she is called Locki, a mere shortening, or rapid pronunciation, I imagine, of her common name.

But, excepting figuratively, as the goddess of fortune, I do not see why she should be deemed fickle, for she is always seen with her

Lord: when reposing on Seshnaga she is shampooing his feet. In the Vishnu Avatara of Rama, Lakshmi was incarnated in the person of the adopted daughter of Raja Janaka, and became Sita, the most faithful spouse of her heroic lord. In the Avatara of Krishna she was Rukmani, the most beloved of the amorous deity. In all the other incarnations of Vishnu, whether Avatara or Avantara, i.e., superior or inferior, she appears, if he had a wife, to have been with him; and mostly under her own name of Lakshmi.

The Hindu women, in imitation and in honour of Lakshmi, bathe with particular ceremonies on certain days; such ceremonies, piously performed on the third day of the light half of the moon Jaishtha, which day is called Rambha Tritiya, are peculiarly auspicious to female beauty—Rambha bathed on that day.

On the third day after that before mentioned, that is the sixth day of the moon's age, which is called Aranya-shashti, women walk in the forests with a fan in one hand, and eat certain vegetables, in hope of beautiful children.

On the dark last day of the moon, Aswina, ceremonies of a peculiar and two-fold nature are performed in honour of both Lakshmi and Bhavani. A fast all day, and a great festival at night, in honour of Lakshmi, with illuminations on trees and houses. Invocations are made at the same time to Kuvera. Here appears a greater connection between these ill-assorted personages than is seen on other occasions. Riches or prosperity is the object of the invocations, and the presiding deities are of course conjoined.

On this night, when the gods, having been delivered by Kesava, were slumbering on the rocks that bounded the sea of milk, Lakshmi, no longer fearing the Daityas, slept apart on a lotus.

I extract a passage from the first volume of the *Asiatic Researches*, descriptive of Lakshmi:

"The Hindus have also their Goddess of Abundance, whom they usually call Lakshmi; and whom they consider as the daughter not of Manu, but of Bhrigu, by whom the first code of sacred ordinances was promulgated. She is also named Padma and Kamala, from the sacred lotus; but her most remarkable name is **Sri, or, in the first case, Sris, which has a resemblance to the Latin Ceres**, and means fortune, or prosperity."

Sir William Jones has addressed a hymn to Lakshmi, "The World's Great Mother," that cannot be perused by an oriental student without great profit; Lakshmi, or Sri, the Ceres of India, the preserving power of nature; or in the language of allegory, the consort of Vishnu or Hari, a personification of divine goodness. Some represent her as the daughter of Bhrigu, a son of Brahma; but in the *Markandeya Purana*, nature is said to have assumed three transcendent forms, according to her three qualities, and each of them to have produced a pair of divinities: Brahma and Lakshmi, Mahesha and Saraswati, Vishnu and Kali. After whose intermarriage, Brahma and Saraswati formed the mundane egg, which Mahesa and Kali divided into halves, and Vishnu, together with Lakshmi, preserved it from destruction. A third story supposes her to have sprung from the sea of milk, when it was churned on the second incarnation of Hari, who is often painted reclining on the serpent Ananta, the emblem of eternity; and this fable, whatever may be the meaning of it, has been chosen as the most poetical:

"Not long inswath'd the sacred infant lay,
(Celestial forms full soon their prime attain):
Her eyes, oft darted o'er the liquid way,
With golden light emblaz'd the darkling main;
And those firm breasts, whence all our comforts well,
Rose with enchanting swell;
Her loose hair with the bounding billows play'd,
And caught in charming toils each pearly shell
That, idling, through the surgy forest stray'd;
When ocean suffer'd a portentous change,
Toss'd with convulsion strange:
For lofty Mandar from his base was torn,
With streams, rocks, woods—by gods and demons whir'd,
While round his craggy sides the mad spray curl'd
Huge mountain! by the passive tortoise borne,

Then sole, but not forlorn,
Shipp'd in a flower, that balmy sweets exhal'd,
O'er dulcet waves of cream Padmaja sail'd:
So name the Goddess, from her lotus blue,
Or Kamala, if more auspicious deem'd;
With many-petal'd wings the blossom flew,
And from the mount a flutt'ring sea-bird seem'd,
Till on the shore it stopp'd—the heav'n-lov'd shore,
Bright with-unvalu'd store
Of gems marine, by mirthful Indra wore;
But she (what brighter gem had shone before?)
No bride for old Maricha's frolic son,
On azure Hari fix'd her prosp'ring eyes.
Love bade the bridegroom rise;
Straight o'er the deep, then dimpling smooth, he rush'd,
And tow'rd th' unmeasur'd snake-stupendous bed!
The world's great mother, not reluctant, led:
All nature glow'd whene'er she smil'd or blush'd;
The king of serpents hush'd
His thousand heads, where diamond mirrors blaz'd,
That multiply'd her image as he gaz'd,"

The Holy Cow

In the Sraddha, or obsequies in honour of deceased ancestors, Lakshmi is, among most other deities, earnestly invoked; particularly when a votary, by gifts to Brahmins, is "desirous of obtaining celestial bliss for the defunct." A denotion of a milch cow is attended by many appropriate ceremonies, finishing with the following prayers, the accepter holding during the recital the sacred animal by the tail:

"May the goddess, who is the Lakshmi of all beings, and resides among the gods, assume the shape of a milch cow, and procure me comfort.

"May she, who is Lakshmi reposing on the bosom of Vishnu; she, who is the Lakshmi of the regent of riches; she, who is the Lakshmi of kings, be a boon-granting cow to me.

"I invoke the goddess who is endowed with the attributes of all the gods, who confers all happiness, who bestows abodes in all the worlds, for the sake of all people.

"I pray to that auspicious goddess for immortality and happiness."

The boon-granting cow so honoured is called Surabhi; and her descendants are much revered by all classes of Hindus. It is common for Brahmins and others to feed a cow before they take their own breakfast:

"Daughter of Surabhi, framed of five elements, auspicious, pure, holy—sprung from the sun, accept this food given by me: salutation unto thee!" Or, if he conducts the kine to grass: "May cows, who are mothers of the three worlds, and daughters of Surabhi, and who are beneficent, pure, and holy, accept the food given by me."7

The Hindus hope to obtain the favour of the boon-granting cow by showing kindness to her and her offspring; and adoration of a cow is not uncommon, such as presenting flowers to her, washing her feet, etc. Many instances of affectionate tenderness for cows and calves have come under my notice, and many stories are beautifully told in Hindu poetics, of boons obtained by those means.

The time is not, perhaps very remote when the original extreme utility of the cow in well peopled and agricultural countries will almost necessarily give rise to a repugnance at slaying them, which will in time grow to stronger prohibitory feelings, and at length be stamped with the sanction of holiness.

It is a curious fact, that the Chinese make no use of milk, either crude, nor in the shape of curds, butter, or cheese (even in Japan—Ed.). Chinese have of course no repugnance at killing cows, nor indeed to killing and eating anything else. **Among the dainties of a Chinese market I have noticed horseflesh, dogs, cats, hawks, crows, owls, etc., offered as edibles. Nor is it very uncommon to see a Chinese pick the lice off his garments and eat them.**

Many writers have noticed the veneration the Hindus have for cows and calves; the custom, so universal in India, of **using cow dung for covering for floors and walls,** it is used for floors by all sects, as well as Hindus, as **the most cool and cleanly article**. This is done, not only in tents and temporary houses of gentlemen, but sometimes over the best apartments of splendid habitations of Europeans as well as natives. **The smell quickly goes off; and no floor is so cool and comfortable, nor so obnoxious to fleas and vermin.** This pleasant and salutary article is falling into disuse with the English, who, in their habitations and habits, are departing more and more from the sober dictates of nature.

We now, for instance, build lofty rooms. admitting insufferable glare and heat through long glazed windows fronting the sun reflected by marble or polished floors; domestic comfort is sacrificed to exterior decoration. No man of taste would now build a low sun-excluding veranda, nor mitigate the intensity of the heat by a cow-dung flooring. The church will now be, like our new houses, insufferably hot; and the adaptation of Pankhas, monstrous fans, ten, twenty, thirty, or more, feet long, suspended from the ceiling of sitting-rooms, and moved to and fro by men outside by means of ropes and pullies, will be necessary. The idea is taken from the natives. I have mythological pictures where persons are seated under them.

Cow-dung is plastered over the cooking-place before the meal of a person of a high class be cooked; in camps, or on journeys, a space of ten or twelve square feet is so purified, and is easily polluted by the approach of impure persons or things, in which case the food becomes unholy. **The ashes of cow-dung are also of a very purifying nature;** and Hindus, occasionally, or frequently, use them, mixed sometimes with other ingredients, to mark their foreheads, necks, and arms. Sometimes men, especially holy beggars or penitents, or those having some claims to sanctity, are rubbed all over with these ashen mixtures, and make a curious sky-blue appearance.

But the greatest, or, at any rate, **the most convenient, of all, purifiers is the urine of a cow;** the catholic devil himself cannot, as the proverb runs, hate holy water more than the Hindu spirits of impurity abhor this sin-expelling sanctifying liquid. Images are sprinkled with it; no man of any pretensions to piety or cleanliness would pass a cow in the act of staling without receiving the holy stream in his palm, sipping a few drops; and, with bedewed fingers marking and crossing his forehead, shoulders, and breasts, in the same manner as papists do.

To strangers it is diverting enough to witness this spiritual sip; and it may be seen at the Bazar Gate, in Bombay, almost any morning at sunrise: cows and buffaloes are daily brought and people resort, thither, for milk. The buffalo is, however, in all points held in far less estimation by Hindus than the cow; and the ingredient in question is by no means equally revered when proceeding from the buffaloes. If the animal be retentive, a pious expectant will impatiently apply his finger, and by judicious tickling excite the grateful flow; if heedless, however, he may perhaps, by super excitation, receive a greater boon than the "descendant of Surabhi" was implored to yield.

Parvati

Of the many names of the goddess that we are about to introduce, more particularly, those of Parvati, Bhavani, Durga, Kali, and Devi, or the Goddess, are the most common.

Although, in the present age, human sacrifices are perhaps no longer made, there can be no doubt of the existence of the practice formerly. To Bhavani, in her character of Kali, it would appear they were chiefly offered; and no religious rite can be more minutely ordained and detailed than this is in the *Kalika Purana*. As well as the ceremonies, the implements, prayers, etc., used on these horrid occasions, are minutely described and recited.

"Let the sacrificer say Hrang, Hring! Kali, Kali! O horrid-toothed goddess! eat, cut, destroy all the malignant—cut with this axe; bind, bind; seize, seize; drink blood; spheng, spheng! secure, secure. Salutation to Kali"—thus ends the Kalaratriya Mantra.

Different mantras are used, in reference to the description of the victim to be immolated; if a lion, this—

"O Hari! who, in the shape of a lion, bearest Chandika, bear my evils, and avert my misfortunes. Thy shape, O lion! was assumed by Hari to punish the wicked part of the human race; and under that form, by truth, the Hiranya-kasipu was destroyed."

Females are not to be immolated, except on very particular occasions; the human female never. An enemy may be immolated by proxy, substituting a buffalo or a goat, and calling the victim by the name of the enemy through the whole ceremony, thereby infusing, by holy texts, the soul of the enemy into the body of the victim; which will, when immolated, deprive the foe of life also. On this occasion—

"Let the sacrificer say, O goddess of horrid form! O Chandika! eat, devour, such a one, my enemy. O consort of Fire! salutation to fire. This is the enemy who has done me mischief, now personated by an animal—destroy him, O Mahamari! spheng, spheng! eat, devour!"

Although human sacrifices were formerly legal, they are most pointedly prohibited in very ancient books; such prohibition is, indeed, a farther proof of the existence of the practice. In the *Brahma Purana* every Naramedha or man-sacrifice, is expressly forbidden; and, in the fifth book of the *Bhagavat,* Sir William Jones has pointed out the following emphatical words: "Whatever men in this world sacrifice human victims, and whatever women eat the flesh of male cattle,

Parvati, Consort of Siva

those men and those women shall the animals here slain torment in the mansions of Yama; and, like slaughtering giants having cleaved their limbs with axes, shall quaff their blood."

Kali, Parvati, Bhavani, and Devi, are names of the same goddess, or Sakti or personisation of an energy in different characters; the name, Parvati, is that borne by the goddess as immediate companion or associate of her divine partner. Were she, when seen in the act of transfixing the demon Mahishasur, to be called Parvati, or Bhavani or perhaps any name but Durga, or Devi, it would not be appropriate; and, of these two names, Durga is the most correct. Again, neither of these epithets are usually applied to her when she is Kali, the Sakti, or active energy of all-renewing Time. Under her name of Bhavani she is said to designate the general of fecundity.

Paolino says, that "Siva and Parvati produced Ganesha, Kartikeya, or Skanda, Hanuman, and Bhagvati," and "that Bhagvati is a gold coin, with the figure of that goddess." To Bhagvati, he says, the house-cock is dedicated and presented at the door of her temple as offering. In the time of infectious diseases, which Indians ascribe to this goddess, their priests and fortune-tellers sometimes slaughter a cock and mutter over certain forms of prayer, such as "Om Bhadrakali namah!" that is "Adoration to thee, O goddess! thou who art black and good." "Thou offended angry deity;" "O woman! with the five visages;" "O goddess! who art formed like a wild swine."

I have attanded ceremonies and sacrifices in Malabar, where a cock was the victim immolated. Women at certain periods, whether monthly, or after delivery, or miscarriage, are purified by such a procedure. Young Malabar females have visitations of the devil as they term it, and are not to be cleasned but by public exorcism. I have been invited to this process, which, in common language, was termed "beating the devil out"; the ceremonies were long, tiresome, and clamorous from drums, trumpets, and shouting. The possessed girl sat quietly, perhaps for several hours, with dishevelled hair, surrounded by her relations, supporting in both palms a pan, said to contain blood. At length, exhausted by fatigue, or roused into hysteria by the noise and tumult, she went into a fit, when the cock's head was cut off close by her. The struggle of the evil spirit in resisting the exorcism are supposed to cause the convulsive agonies of the possessed, in the excess of which it passes into the cock, and is dismissed by his decapitation. These matters are always performed in the night, and are attended with considerable expense for priests, music, etc.

Siva, as the consort of Kali, is Kala; sometimes, however we see Kali as a distinct personage, and the devourer of Siva, as well as of Brahma and Vishnu.

Paterson says: "Maha Kali, black and dreadful, is encompassed by symbols of destruction; two of her hands seem employed in the work of death; of the other two, one appears pointing downwards, alluding to the universal havoc which surrounds her, while the other, pointing upwards, seems to promise the regeneration of nature by a new creation.

"Maha Kali is represented without a crescent (the artificial measure of Time), because it is unnecessary to her character as the hieroglyphic of eternity; but the belief of the Hindus in successive destruction and renovations of the universe accounts for her wearing a Mundmala, or necklace of skulls, as emblems of those revolutions."

When Kala, or Time, shall have devoured all things, the three personified powers will likewise cease to exist; and Kala devouring himself, will then also cease to be. Descending into such depths of abstract metaphysics, some confusion of ideas and persons must arise; but this does not deter the Hindu from endless personisations.

In a passage, Maha Pralaya, or the grand consummation of all things, we see all creation falling, and Brahma, Vishnu, and Siva, about to fall into the "jaws of inexistence." One would have imagined that inexistence might have remained unpersonified; here, however, we see it embodied. The poet, at a loss for words to express so recondite a conception, has necessarily recourse to metaphor for illustration; the painter, at no loss, pursues the allegory, and fills up the ideal outline of the poet.

The name Parvati took its rise from a wild poetical fiction. Himalaya, or the mansion of snow, is the vast chain of mountains that limit India to the north, and embraces it with its eastern and western arms, both extending to the ocean: one named Chandra-sekhara, or the moon's rock; and the other which reaches westward to the mouth of the Indus, called by the ancients Montes Parvati. The mountain Himalaya, being personified, is represented as a powerful monarch, whose wife was Mena; their daughter is named Parvati, or mountain-born, and Durga, or of difficult access. She is said to have been married to Siva in a pre-existing state, when she was named Sati; but she bore no children till she became regenerate in the person of Parvati.

The daughter of Himalaya had two sons: Ganesa, the wisest of deities, always invoked at the beginning of every literary work; and Kartikeya, a commander of the celestial armies.

The following is the last stanza of the hymn:

"O Durga! thou hast deign'd to shield
Man's feeble virtue with celestial might,
Gliding from your jasper field;
And, on a lion borne, has brav'd the fight:
For when the demon Vice thy realms defy'd,
And arm'd with death each arched horn,
Thy golden lance, O goddess! mountain-born,"

The stanza refers to a transfiguration of Bhavani, very commonly met with in pictures and casts. Among mine I have, upwards of a dozen different casts of it in metal, in which the goddess has from two to thirty-two arms, filled with a variety of weapons. I have also several pictures of this subject.

In an in inscription, found in a cave near Gaya, of which a translation is given by Mr. Wilkins, the first lines are:

"When the foot of the goddess was, with its tinkling ornaments, planted upon the head of Mahishasur, all the blossoms of the new-blown flower of the fountain were dispersed with disgrace by its superior beauty. May that foot, radiant with a fringe of refulgent beams issuing from its pure bright nails, endow you with a steady and an unexampled devotion, offered up with fruits, and show you the way to dignity and wealth."

In Mr. Wilkins' introductory letter is the following passage, describing the combat between the monster and Durga, as well as the birth or origin of that form of the goddess.

"The first lines of the first verse allude to the story of Bhavani's killing the evil spirit Mahishasur, who, in the disguise of a buffalo, as the name imparts, had fought with Indra and his celestial bands for a hundred years, defeated him, and usurped his throne; the story is to be found at length in a little book called Chandi. The vanquished spirits, being banished from the heavens, and doomed to

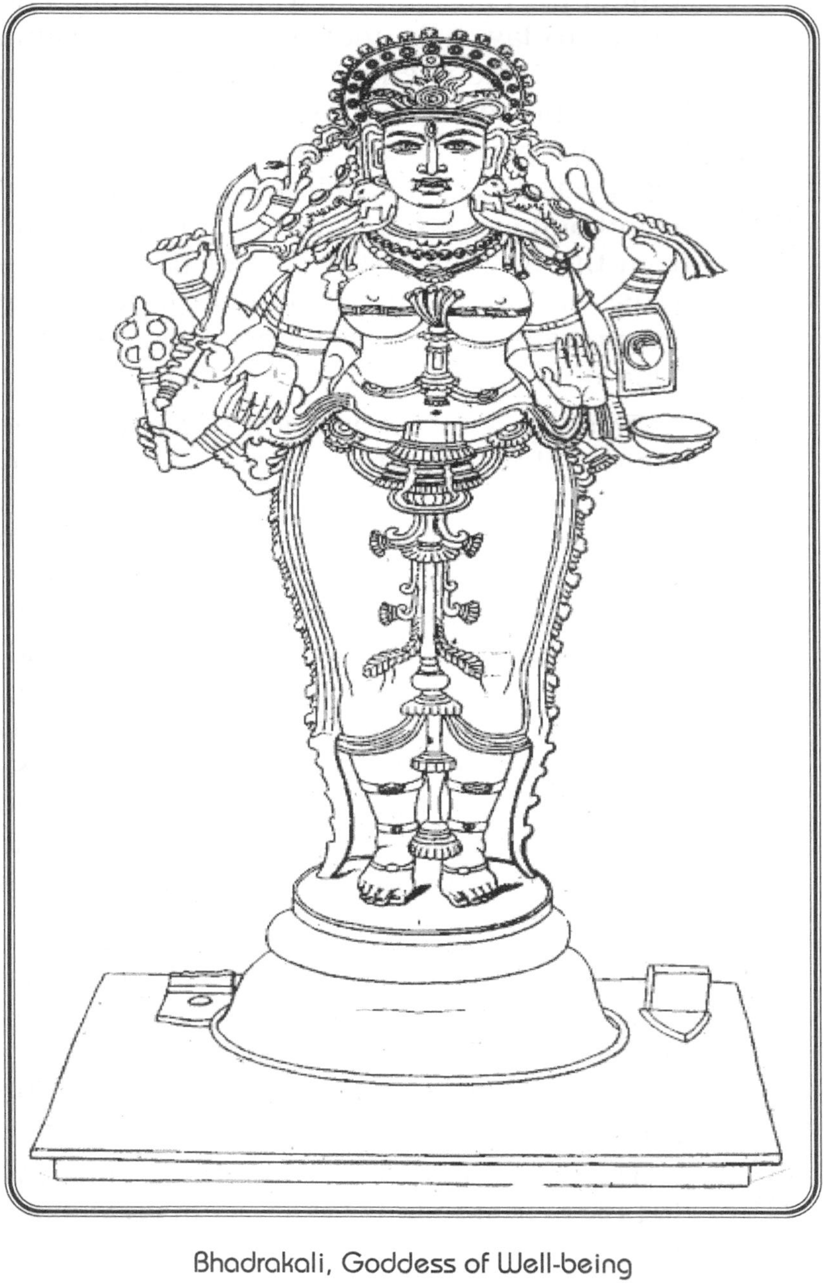

Bhadrakali, Goddess of Well-being

wander the earth, after a while assemble, and resove to lay their grievances before Vishnu and Siva. Conducted by Brahma, they repaired into the presence to those deities, who heard their complaint with compassion; and their anger was so violent against Mahishasura, that a kind of flame issued from their mouths, and from the mouths of the rest of the principal gods: of which was formed a goddess, of inexpressible beauty, with ten arms, and each hand holding a different weapon.

This was a transfiguration of Bhavani, the consort of Siva, under which she is generally called Durga. She is sent against the usurper: she mounts her lion, the gift of the mountain Himalaya, snowy, and attacks the monster, who shifts his form repeatedly; till at length the goddess planteth her foot upon his head, and cuts it off with a single stroke of her sword. Immediately the upper part of a human body issues through the neck of the headless buffalo, and aims a stroke, which being warded off by the lion with his right paw, Durga puts an end to the combat by piercing him through the heart with a spear,"

Katyayani, Kirti, Mahamaya, Shashti, Girja, Uma, are other names of Devi; Gowri is another, meaning fair or young; as does Sudurga. Har-Gowri, like Siva-Parvati, is a title given to the joined deities.

The bright half of the month Aswina, the first of the Hindu lunar year, seems peculiarly devoted to Durga. The first nine nights, called

Navaratri, are, with appropriate names, allotted to her decoration; the fifth is for the preparation of her dress; on the sixth she is awakened; on the seventh she is invited to a bower formed of the leaves of nine plants, of which the Bilwa is the chief. The seventh, eighth, and ninth, are the great days; on the last of which the victims immolated to her honour must be slain, as particularly directed in the Kalika Purana: "The sacrificed beasts must be killed by one blow, with a broad sword or sharp axe."

The next day the goddess is reverently dismissed, and her image is cast into the river, which finishes the festival called Durgotsava and Dasera. On the fifteenth day, that of the full moon, her devotees pass the night in sports and merriment, and games of various sorts; it is unlucky to sleep; for on this night the fiend Nikumbha led his army against Durga, and Lakshmi descended, promising wealth to those who were awake. On this night Kuvera aud Indra are also worshipped.

One of Bhavani's numerous forms is that of Annapurna Devi, meaning the goddess who fills with food. She is a very common household deity. Among my images I have ten of her single and several others in groups. Several of my images are less than an inch, and no one more than three inches in height; some have the appearance of having been buried.

It cannot be doubted that the Anna Perenna of the Romans was the same deity; authorities are adduced in proof by Mr.

Paterson and Mr. Colebrooke She is, Mr. Paterson says, represented sitting on a throne, giving food with a golden ladle to an infant Siva.

At Tuljapur, a respectable town in the Maratha country, between Poona and Hyderabad, the goddess has, I am told, a temple, and is much worshipped in the neighbourhood; whence the name of the town is sometimes given to her as an epithet and she is called Tuljapuri. An ear of corn is said to be in one of her hands. Yenkuba and Ganesa, the latter often called Ganpati, the former is a deity, or saint, of local celebrity, not being chronicled sacred in ancient books. Devi is tiger-mounted, thence named Vyaghra-yani.

• • •

3

Vedic Deities: Indra, Varuna, Surya, Chandra, Agni

Indra

Sir Willam Jones has addressed a hymn to Indra, replete with mythological allusions, and embellished with all the charms of poetry. He says:

"Indra, or the king of immortals, corresponds with one of the ancient Jupiters, for several of that name were worshipped in Europe; and particularly with Jupiter the conductor, whose attributes are so nobly described by the Platonic philosophers.

"He may be considered as the Jove of Ennius, in his memorable line: 'Aspice hoc sublime candens, quem invocant omnes Jovem,' where the poet clearly means the firmament, of which Indra is the personification. He is the God of Thunder, and of nature's elements, with inferior genii under his command; and is conceived to govern the eastern quarter of the world, but to preside, like the Genius, or Agathodoemon, of the ancients, over the celestial bands, stationed on the summit of Meru, where he solaces the gods with nectar and heavenly music.

" The genii, named Kinnara, are the male dancers in Swarga, the heaven of Indra; and the Apsaras are his dancing girls."

Indra resides in the celestial city of Amaravati, where his palace, Vaijayanta, is situated in the garden Nandana, which contains the all-yielding trees Pariyataka, Kalpadruma, and three others similarly beautiful. Although these or even one of them, might suffice, and qualify its owner for the title which Indra bears of Lord of wealth, he is sometimes represented to assess likewise the all-prolific cow, Kamdhenu, as well as Uchchaisrava, the eight-headed horse that arose with the cow and the first-named tree from the churned ocean, as related in another place. His consort is Indrani; he rides the elephant Airavata, driven by his charioteer Matali; and he holds the weapon Vajra, or the thunderbolt, and is hence named Vajrapani. His chief musician is named Chitraratha, who rides in a painted car, which on one occasion was burned by Arjun, the confidential friend of Krishna, or the Sun. Indra is more especially the regent of winds and showers; the water-spout is said to be the trunk of his elephant; and the iris is appropriately called his bow, which it is not deemed auspicious to paint out.

Indra, as well as the deity presiding over the firmament, and over atmospheric or meteoric phenomena, is himself, as are most

Indra, the God of Thunder

of the minor deities, a star, or a constellation: his name is among the twelve Adityas, or Suns.

He is fabled to have lost for a while his kingdom to the Asuras, which are in fact the stars of the southern hemisphere, under the dominion of Yama; who holds his court In the antarctic circle, and is at frequent war with Indra and the Suras, in the northern hemisphere; the metropolis of which is Meru, the Olympus of Indra, the celestial north pole, allegorically represented as a mountain of gold and gems. Deeming the Suras and Asuras to be the stars in the two hemispheres, I apprehend that some astronomical fact is veiled in the allegory of Indra's dethronement: the precession of the equinoxes, perhaps, or annual motion of the stars from east to west, by which Indra has his stellar locality usurped by some other luminary.

In his wars he employs many elephants, which, in reality, are clouds. The chief of all is Airavat, it being his vahan or vehicle: the name means watery, the aqueous property of clouds being most apparent.

The Hindus have assigned regents to each cardinal and intermediate point of the compass. Indra is esteemed the first of firmamental deities, and especially the ruler of the east, that point is reckoned first, and the others are thus ruled: Agni, south-east; Yama, south; Nirit, south-west; Varuna, west; Vayu, north-west; Kuvera, north; and Isana, north-east. To which are sometimes added three other quarters, or points, above, governed by Brahma; below, by Naga, or Seshnaga, the king of serpents, otherwise named Vasuki; and the centre, ruled by Rudra, or Siva.

Here we find Brahma and Siva in situations apparently subordinate to Indra; Siva, indeed, holds two offices, being as Isa, or Isani, governor of the north-east region; and as Rudra, of the central district. But they are both confessedly superior to Indra, who is generally esteemed prince of the beneficent genii; and is, like his betters, an extraordinary and equivocal character, as will appear in this sequel. He is poetically described as

"It Mounted on the Sun's bright beam"—
"Darter of the swift blue bolt"—
"Sprinkler of genial dews and fruitful rains
O'er hills and thirsty plains"—

and is called Lord of Wealth, for which a good reason has been already given; beautiful, with a thousand eyes, and the destroyer of towns.

Ahilya was the handsome wife of the pious rishi Gotama. Her beauty attracted the depraved Indra, and he was well nigh succeeding in his adulterous pursuit, but for the intrusion of the holy Gotama, who imprecated this curse upon Indra—that he should be covered with the marks of what had been the object of his lawless desires; which took immediate effect. On the repentance and entreaties of the detected deity, the good man recanted, and mitigated the curse by changing the marks of his shame to as many eyes.

This moderation, on the part of the temperate Sage, had not, its effect on the persevering deity, who, disguising himself in the semblance of the venerable man, succeeded in seducing the austere Ahilya. Gotama again intruded, but malapropos for the frail ones, and thus cursed his unlucky wife: "For an innumerable series of years, O sinful wretch, lie in ashes in a certain forest, enduring excessive pain, and invisible, until the coming of Rama: beholding of whom, thou shalt again, approach Gotama without fear. Indra by the malediction of the Sage became an eunuch, and was overcome with shame and sorrow; but at the intercession of all the gods and the Maruts, with Agni at their head, he was restored to manhood by the Pitris, at the expense of a ram. From such instances of frailty, Indra became proverbial for profligacy.

Indra is an evil counsellor, aiding by his advice the malignant asuras, or any ill-disposed human being, in counteracting the beneficent intentions of the gods, and thwarting the piety of men. Covetous of sacrifices, he sees not without envy and jealousy offerings made to other deities; and when not especially or exclusively dedicated to himself, has been known to steal the victim, or some essential sacrificial utensil. At an Aswamedha, he will steal the horse, for the whole year previous to its immolation. In the Ramayana it is related how Indra stole from the sacred pile the victim of the king, Ambarisha, who resolving on a human sacrifice, had consecrated a man, appointed for the immolation. And elsewhere it is stated how Indra, in a rage occasioned by hunger, killed his friend and companion Namuchi.

Indra, however, might well be satisfied with his allowed portion of sacrificial propitiation; for he is very frequently and, in point of precedence, honorably, invoked in many Brahmanical ceremonies. At the Sraddha, or obsequies in honour of deceased ancestors, the priest, meditating the Gayatri, says,

"May Indra and Varuna accept our oblations, and grant us happiness; may Indra and the cherishing Sun grant us happiness in the distribution of food; may Indra and the Moon grant us the happiness of attaining the road of celestial bliss, and the association of good offices."

And the same gentleman, in his most valuable Essay on the Vedas, describes from that fruitful source a supposed consecration of Indra, when elected by the gods to be their king. I extract the concluding paragraph:

"Thus consecrated by that great inauguration, Indra subdued all conquerable earths, and won all worlds; he obtained over all the gods supremacy, transcendent rank, and pre-eminence. Conquering in this world below, equitable dominion, separate authority, attainment of the supreme abode, mighty power, and superior rule; becoming a self-existent being, and independent ruler, exempt from early dissolution; and reaching all his wishes in that celestial world, he became immortal; he became immortal."

In the *Book of Manu*, the component parts of a king are enumerated; among which Indra obtains a place:

"The corporeal frame of a king is composed of particles from Soma, Agni, Surya, Pavana, Indra, Kuvera, Varuna, and Yama, the eight guardian deities of the world."

In the marriage ceremony, after eighteen oblations are offered, while as many texts are meditated, they differ only in the name of the deity invoked.

"May Agni, lord of living beings, protect me in respect of holiness, valour, and prayer, and in regard to ancient privileges, to this solemn rite, and to this invocation to deities.— May Indra, lord, or regent, of the eldest that is, of the best of beings, protect me, etc."

The eight guardian deities of the eight points of the heavens, with Indra at their head, are sometimes called the winds, and almost confounded with the Maruts, of whom, however, are reckoned forty-nine.

Indra is generally represented on his elephant, he is so seen in the Elephanta cavern, and in the excavations at Ellora. Like the other Hindu deities, Indra is distinguished by several names: Sakra is that by which he is generally called in his capacity of the adviser of evil. Shatkratu means him to whom is made a hundred sacrifices; Vritrahana, the slayer of the demon Vritra; Upendra, inferring subordination to Indra who is sometimes named Mahendra, or the great Indra; also Purendra, and Vasava, and Pakshasana. Vajrapani means grasper of the thunderbolt. His consort, Indrani, is also named Poulomi and Sachi.

I shall now notice some of those subordinate to Indra as chief of the demigods, and immediately connected with him as regents of quarters, or points, or winds; and some of them that do not demand any lengthened discussion: Varuna, Kuvera and Nirrit.

Varuna

Varuna is the regent of the ocean, and generally of large masses of water. As light is thought to be excluded from the depths of water, Varuna is also deemed the governor of the night, or of darkness; still he is one of the Adityas, or Suns. **He is likewise styled the lord of punishment;** and in this character the wealth of criminals is directed to be offered to him, or, in other words, thrown into the waters; or it may, instead, be bestowed on a learned priest: the latter, we may suppose, is likely to outshare the deity.

The *Book of Manu* says:

"Let no virtuous prince appropriate the wealth of a criminal in the highest degree; for he who appropriates it through covetousness, is contaminated with the same guilt.

"Having thrown such a fine into the waters, let him offer it to Varuna; or let him bestow it on some priest of eminent learning in the scriptures.

"Varuna is the lord of punishment; he holds a rod even over kings; and a priest who has gone through the whole Veda is equal to a sovereign of the world."

In another quotation from Manu, this passage occurs: "Varuna most assuredly binds the guilty in fatal cords." And the cord of Varuna called Pasha, or Varunapasha, is frequently spoken of, which he is supposed to hold in his hand; but I have no image or picture of this deity.

In the Black Yajurveda, an Upanishad is named after Varuna; he is there made the father of Bhrigu, and is introduced as instructing his son in the mysteries of religious science, particularly as to the nature of Brahman; who is, he says, "That, whence all beings are produced; that, by which they live when born; that, toward which they tend; and that, unto which they pass."

Bhrigu, after meditating in devout contemplation, recognised food to be Brahman: "for all beings are indeed produced from food; when born they live by food; toward food they tend; and they pass into food."

Unsatisfied, however, he, again deeply meditating, discovered breath to be Brahman: "for all beings are indeed produced from breath; when born they live by breath; toward breath they tend; they pass into breath."

Again desired to seek Brahman in profound meditation, he discovered intellect to be Brahman: "for all these beings are produced from intellect; when born they live by intellect; toward intellect they tend; and they pass into intellect."—This he understood; but again coming to his father Varuna, saying, "Venerable father, make known to me Brahman"—Varuna replied, "Inquire by devout contemplation, profound meditation, what is Brahman."

He thought deeply, and having thus meditated with devout contemplation, he knew Ananda (or felicity) to be Brahman: "for all these beings are indeed produced from pleasure; when born they live by joy; they tend toward happiness; they pass into felicity."

"Such is the science which was attained by Bhrigu, taught by Varuna, and founded on the supreme ethereal spirit: he who knows this, rests on the same support; is endowed with abundant food, and becomes a blazing fire which consumes food; great is he by progeny, by cattle, and by holy perfections; and great by propitious celebrity."

Varuna is the special protector of the west point of the heavens: he has a Sakti, or consort named Varuni. She is sometimes called his daughter. He is one of the Adityas, or Suns, the offspring of Aditi. But, although he is one of the main deities invoked and propitiated in the daily ceremonies of the Brahmins, his name does not very often occur in Hindu writings or conversaion.

Kuvera

Kuvera, the regent of wealth, now demands our attention; and although few people seek the favour of this deity with greater avidity than the Hindus, yet **I find but little mention of him in my mythological memoranda; nor have I any image or picture of him.** Let us hope that the Indian Plutus will not be for ever withholding his favour, resent my brief notice of him, compared with the more extended account of more social or more amiable deities. On Kama, Lakshmi, or Saraswati, poets and historians dwell with complacency and delight; but **the gloomy, selfish, and deformed Kuvera, claims not, nor perhaps deserves, so much of our attention.**

He is, as we have seen, the guardian of the northern region; described, in respect of externals, as a mere man, but as a magnificent deity residing in the splendid city Alaka, otherwise called Chitraratha; or borne through the sky in a gorgeous car, called Pushpaka. He is also called Vittesa; and Paulastya, a name of one of the Brahmadikas; also Visravana, or Vaisrava, and Dhanada. He is said to be the son of a sage Visrava, or Viswasrava; the father also of Ravana, who, as well as Kuvera, is hence called Visravana. Kuvera and Ravana are thus half-brothers, having different mothers: both are occasionally named Paulastya.

His servants and companions are the Yakshas and Guhyakas, into whose forms transmigrate the souls of those men who in this life are addicted to sordid and base passions, or absorbed in worldly prosperity. We happily do not find that the regent of wealth is related in marriage or otherwise with Lakshmi, the goddess of riches, to whom, a Hindu, would address himself for that boon, and not to Kuvera.

Nirrit

Nirrit, otherwise called Nairita and Nirut; and sometimes Virupaksha, meaning, it is said, with three eyes; but, with a disagreeable countenance. His name occurs but seldom in writing or conversation; and I have no image or picture of him, nor did I ever see one. His consort is Nirriti, who seems to share with him the honour of his government; and a man becoming criminal on certain points, it is incumbent on him to "sacrifice a black or a one-eyed ass, by way of a meal offering to Nirriti, patroness of the south-west, by night, in a place where four ways meet."

Surya

Surya, the glorious god of day holding the attributes of Vishnu, seated on a seven-headed serpent; his car drawn by a seven-headed horse, driven by the legless Arun, a personification of the dawn, or Aurora.

So grand a symbol of the deity, as the Sun "looking from his sole dominion like the god or this world," which, to ignorant people, must be his most glorious and natural type, will of course have attracted the earliest adoration; and where revelation was withheld, will almost necessarily have been the primary fount of idolatry. The investigators of ancient mythology accordingly trace to this prolific source, wherein they are melted and lost, almost ever other mythological personage; who, like his own light, diverge and radiate from his most glorious centre.

A hymn sings:

"Lord of the lotus, father, friend, and king,
Surya, thy powers I sing
Thy substance, Indra, with his heavenly bands,
Nor sings. nor understands.
Nor e'en the Vedas three to man explain
Thy mystic orb triform, the Brahma tun'd the strain.

"First o'er blue hills appear.
With many an agate hoof.
And pasterns fring'd with pearl, seven coursers green.
Nor boasts yon arched woof,
That girds the show'ry sphere,
Such heav'n-spun threads of colour'd light serene.
As tinge the reins which Arun guides—
Glowing with immortal grace,
Young Arun. loveliest of Vinatian race;
Though younger he, whom Madhava bestrides,
When high on eagle-plumes he rides.

Surya, the Sun

But, Oh! what pencil of a living star
Could paint that gorgeous car,
In which as in an ark, supremely bright,
The lord of boundless light,
Ascending calm o'er the empyrean sails,
And with ten thousand beams his awful beauty veils!"

Surya is believed to have descended frequently from his car in a human shape, and to have left a race on earth, who are equally renowned in Indian stories with the Heliades of Greece. It is very singular that his two sons, called Aswinikumara in the dual, should be considered as twin brothers Esculapius among the gods, and are believed to have been born of a nymph who in the form of a mare, was impregnated with sunbeams. I suspect the whole fable of Kasyapa and his progeny to be astronomical; and cannot but imagine that the Greek name Cassiopeia has relation to it.

Surya in his car, drawn by seven horses, driven by Arun, or the dawn; and he is described as followed by thousands of genii, worshipping him, and modulating his praises. He has a multitude of names, and among them twelve epithets, or titles, which denote his distinct powers in each of the twelve months; those powers are called Adityas, or sons of Aditi, by Kasyapa, the Indian Uranus; and one of them has, according to some authorities, the name of Vishnu, or Pervader,

Vishnu is doubtless one of the epithets of the Sun, in whom will be found to merge all the idolatrous machinery of all systems of mythology.—"Here it must be observed," as quoted in another place, "that at night, and in the west, the Sun is Vishnu: he is Brahma in the east, and in the morning, from noon to evening, he is Siva."

Another picture represents the Hindu zodiac and solar system, called Rasi Chakra. Here we see Surya in the centre, surrounded in the first circle by the planetary orbs; Chandra, Mangala, or Mars, Buddha, or Mercury, Vrihaspati, or Jupiter, Sukra, or Venus, Sani, or Saturn, Rahu and Ketu, the ascending and descending nodes.

I will now extract the sacrificial prayers to the nine charactres named in the paragraph, introduced into the rites of the oblation to Fire; part of the worship offered to the gods, and one of the five daily sacraments of a Brahmin; with each prayer an oblation of ghee is made:

"The Divine Sun approaches with his golden car, returning alternately with the shades of night, ruling mortal and immortal beings, and surveying the world.—May this oblation to Surya be efficacious.

"Gods! produce that Moon which has no foe, which is the son of the solar orb, and become the offering of space, for the benefit of this world, produce it for the advancement of knowledge, for protection from danger, for vast supremacy, for empire, and for the sake of Indra's organs of sense.—May this oblation to Chandra be efficacious.

"This gem of the sky, whose head resembles fire, is the lord of waters, and replenishes the seeds of the earth.—May this oblation to Mangala be efficacious.

"Be roused, O Fire! and thou O Budha! perfect this sacrificial rite, and associate with us; let this votary, and all the gods, sit in this most excellent assembly.—May this oblation be efficacious.

"O Vrihaspati! sprung from eternal truth, confer on us abundantly that various wealth which the most venerable of beings may revere; which shines glorious among all people, which serves to defray sacrifices, which is preserved by strength.—May this oblation be efficacious.

"The lord of creatures drank the invigorating essence distilled from food; he drank milk and the juice of the moon-plant. By means of scripture, which is truth itself, the beverage thus quaffed became a prolific essence, the eternal organ of universal perception, Indra's organs of sense, the milk of immortality, and honey to the manes of ancestors.—May this oblation to Sukra be efficacious."

"May divine waters be auspicious to us for accumulation, for gain, and for refreshing draughts; may they listen to us, that we may be associated with good auspices.—May this oblation to Sani be efficacious.

"O Durva! which doth germinate at every knot, at every joint, multiply us through a hundred, through a thousand, descents.—May *this oblation to Rahu the planet of the ascending code be efficacious.*

"Be thou produced by dwellers in this world to give knowledge to ignorant mortals, and wealth to the indigent, or beauty to the ugly.—May this oblation to Ketu, the planet of the descending node be efficacious."

The great family, called "Children of the Moon," is so named in contradistinction from another race, called "Children of the Sun." They are severally called Surya-vansa and Chandra-vansa; both families are, in the theogony of the Hindus, deducible from Brahma.

In a note, Chandra is made the offspring of Atri, who was a son of Brahma. Chandra's son, Budha, married Ila, daughter of Manu: hence originated the Chandra-vansa.

The Surya-vansa, or offspring of the Sun, also proceed from this seventh Manu, who is fabled to be the son of Surya; one of whose names is Vaivaswat; thence named Vaivaswata. Surya is the son of Kasyapa (or Uranus), the son of Marichi (or light), the son of Brahma.

In the Gayatri, the Sun is called Savitri; as he is also in an invocation to diverse deities in marriage ceremonies, as extracted under Indra but not apparently as a female; indeed, in the latter instance, decidedly not, as he is especially styled "Savitri, the Generative Sun, lord of pregnant females." Sir William Jones marks a day in the Calendar, called "Savitri Vratam", as "a fast, with ceremonies by women at the roots of the Indian fig tree, to preserve them from widowhood."

Mr. Colebrooke says: "The seventh chapter of the tenth boof of the Rig Veda opens with a hymn, in which Surya, surnamed Savitri, the wife of the Moon, is made the speaker, as Dakshina, daughter of Prajapati, and Juhu, daughter of Brahma, are in subsequent chapters." This marriage is noticed in the *Aitareya Brahmana,* where the second lecture of the fourth book opens in this manner: 'Prajapati gave his daughter Surya Savitri to Soma the king."

In the oriental zodiac, the planets are accommodated with vehicles: Surya is on a lion, and Arun is beneath him, driving the seven-headed horse yoked to the empty car; Chandra is riding an antelope; Mangala is on a horse, with a huge sabre in his hand: Budha rides an eagle; Vrihaspati a boar and holds apparently a book; Sukra holds a disk, and rides a camel; Sani is mounted on an elephant; the headless Rahu holds a spear, and stands on a tortoise; and Ketu, his head, is borne by a frog.

Soma as a name of the Moon is almost as common as Chandra; and the day Monday, Somvar, has received its designation from the name.

The names of Surya are numerous: Aryama, Vivaswat, Martanda, Sura, Ravi, Mihira, Bhanu, Arka, Haridaswa, Karmasakshi Savitri, Pushan, Bhaskara, Tapana, Twashti, Bhaga, Mitra, Heli,

Varuna, Vedanga, Indra, Gabhasti, Yama, Vishnu, Krishna.

Prabha, or Brightness, is the consort of the glorious luminary Surya; and that, unable to sustain the pressure of his intensity, she once assumed a form named Chhaya, or Shade, and was impregnated by him; this personification of shade is sometimes called the wife of Surya.

Enthusiastic devotees are encouraged to penances in honour of different deities. Gazing on the Sun, a mode of moving Surya's favour, must be exceedingly hurtful and distressing; it a very uncommon penance in these days.

The dawn, the precursor of Surya, or the Sun, is personified in Arun, who may be styled the Aurora of the Hindus. Arun, or Aruna, is the charioteer of Surya.

Chandra

Chandra, the regent of the Moon, appears in a car drawn by pied antelopes; his head encircled by a crescent, and sometimes with a rabbit on his banner. Although he has one or more of the usual emblems of Vishnu he seems still, in a greater degree, connected with Siva, who is often seen moon-crowned; and has hence the epithet of Chandra-sekhara: he is also frequently seen with Chandra's emblem, the antelope.

The god Soma or Chandra, was traversing the earth with his favourite consort Rohini and arriving at the southern mountain, Sahyadri, they unwarily entered the forest of Gauri, where some men having surprised Mahadeva caressing that goddess, had been formerly punished by a change of their sex and the forest had retained a power of effecting a like change on all males who should enter it. Chandra, instantly becoming a female was so afflicted and ashamed, that she hastened far to the west, sending Rohini to her seat in the sky; and concealed herself in a mountain, afterwards named Soma-giri, where she performed acts of the most rigorous devotion. Darkness then covered the world as night; the fruits of the earth were destroyed; and the universe was in such dismay, that the Devas with Brahma at their head, implored the assistance of Mahadeva, who no sooner placed Chandra on his forehead than she became male again; and hence he acquired the title of Chandrasekhara.

This fable is taken from the Puranas, and is thus explained:

" To the inhabitants of the countries near the source of the Kali, the moon, being in the mansion of Rohini, or the Pleiades, seemed to vanish behind the southern mountains. Now, when the Moon is in opposition to the Sun, it is the god Chandra; but when in conjunction with it, the goddess Chandra, who was in that state feigned to have conceived the Pulindas. The moon is believed by the Hindu naturalists to have a powerful influence on vegetation, especially on certain plants; and above all, on the Somalata, or Moonplant."

Chandra

As well as a solar, the Hindus have a lunar zodiac, divided into twenty-eight mansions, called Nakshatras; and believed to have been so divided, or invented, by Daksha, a mythological son of Brahma; hence their poetical astronomy feign these Nakshatras to be the offspring or daughters of Daksha, and, as diurnally receiving the moon in his ethereal journey, to be the wives of Chandra. Of these wives, Chandra is fabled to have the greatest affection for Rohini, the fourth daughter of Daksha, who, on the complaint cursed Chandra with a consumption that continued for fifteen days; but on his due repentance, his strength and splendour were gradually restored: this story is detailed in the Siva Purana.

I do not find so many names of this fickle deity; Chandra and Soma are the commonest. Indu, Himansu, Sasin, Saganka, and Anumati, are the only varieties of his designations that I find noted.

Agni

Agni is the Hindu regent or personification of Fire. In all my tinted pictures he is painted a deep red. He has two faces, three legs, and seven arms; when mounted, he has a ram as his vahan or vehicle, and his banner bears that animal; from each mouth a forked tongue or flame is seen to issue.

Agni, the God of Fire

His two faces, I imagine, allude to the two fires, solar and terrestrial, or to creative heat and destructive fire; three legs, to the three sacred terrestrial fires of the Brahmins—the nuptial, the ceremonial, and the sacrificial, or to the influence of fire in and over the three regions of the universe; his seven arms were originally derived from the prismatic divisibility of a ray of light; light or heat, and fire, being so immediately connected, we may expect to find a common attribute derived from the same source.

The sacred triad of fires is thus enumerated in the *Book of Manu*:

"Due reverence to those three (the parents and preceptor) is considered as the highest devotion; and without their approbation, no man must perform any other duty.

"Since they alone are held equal to the three worlds; they alone, to the three principal orders; they alone, to the three Vedas; they alone, to the three fires.

"The natural father is considered as the Garhapatya, or nuptial fire; the mother, as the Dakshina, or ceremonial; the spiritual guide, as the Ahavaniya, or sacrificial; this triad of fires is most venerable."

In the ceremony called Viswedeva, or all the gods, the mystical number of seven frequently occurs; in this prayer, for instance, addressed to Agni:

"Fire! seven are thy fuels; seven thy holy sages; seven thy beloved abodes; seven ways do seven sacrificers worship thee; thy sources are seven. Be content with this clarified butter; may this oblation be efficacious."

The seven tongues of fire, are Pravaha, Avaha, Udvaha, Shamvaha, Vivaha, Parivaha, Nivaha (or Anuvaha); all of which imply the power of conveying oblations to the deities to whom offerings are made. The seven holy sages and sacrifices are the Hotri, Maitra-varuna, Brahmanahchhandasi, Achhavaka, Potri, Neshtri, and Agnidhra; that is, the seven officiating priests at very solemn sacrifices. They worship fire seven ways: by the Agnishtoma, and other sacrifices. The seven abodes are the names of the seven worlds; and fire is called in the Veda Saptachitika, which seems to allude to seven consecrated hearths. In the sixteen verses, called Purusha, the names of the seven worlds, thrice repeated, are understood to be meant by the thrice seven fuels; and the seven oceans are the seven moats surrounding the altar. Fire, like the sun itself, is supposed to emit seven rays: this may, perhaps, account for the number seven being so often repeated.

The Vedas are variously subdivided, and certain portions are variously attributed to certain gods and men. To Agni is assigned seven Kandas, or books, of the Yajurveda. One of the Puranas is called the Agni Purana.

Agni had seven brothers, whose names signify flame. By one wife he had three sons—Uttama, Tamasa, Raivata; they became Manus, and their names have, I imagine, some allusions, direct or inverse, to fire, or heat, or light: Tamasa, for instance, is darkness. By another wife, Agni had nine sons; one of his wives was named Swaha, and she is called the goddess of fire, and is invoked on some occasions where she is called "the consuming power of those who eat solemn sacrifices;" that is Fire, she being the Sakti or energy of Agni.

Pavaka, and Agnidhra, are other names of Agni: Pavaka signifies the Purifier. He is also called Anala.

Krishna, describing his own pre-eminence among all things and creatures, says to Arjun: "Among the Vasus I am Pavaka."

Again, speaking of some reform among the ancient Persians, in the eighth or ninth century before Christ, Jones says, that "While they rejected the complex polytheism of their predecessors, they retained the laws of Mahabad, with a superstitious veneration for the sun, the planets, and fire; thus resembled the sects called Sauras and Sagnikas; the second of which is very numerous at Benares, where many Agnihotras are continually burning, and where the Sagnikas, when they enter on their sacerdotal office, kindle, with two pieces of the hard wood Sami, a fire, which they keep lighted through their lives—for their nuptial ceremony, the performance of solemn sacrifices, and the obsequies of departed ancestors, and their own funeral pile. This remarkable rite was continued by Zaratusht, who reformed the old religion by the addition of genii, or angels, presiding over months and days; of new ceremonics in the veneration shown to fire; of a new work which he pretended to have received from heaven; and, above all, by establishing the actual adoration of one Supreme Being."

The fire used by Brahmins for cooking, and for religious ceremonies, is produced by the friction of two pieces of hard wood; one about five inches diameter, with a small conical hole, or sacker, in the upper part, into which the other, shaped like a pin, is introduced, and whirled about backward and forward by a bow; the pin and socket fitting, the great attrition soon produces fire. This machine, is called Arani, and should be made of the Sami tree, it being sacred to Devi, or if that be not procurable, of the Pipala, A particular day is set apart for the festival of Sami Devi, when fires are lighted in the evening under the Sami tree; offerings are made of rice and flowers, and sometimes of spirits; the votaries sing her praise, and in praise of the tree; some of the leaves of which, and some earth, are carried home, and kept till the festival of the ensuing year.

• • •

4

The Ten Avataras

Allusions and references to the Avataras occur so perpetually in all researches into the mythology of the Hindus; and, indeed, nearly all of their history and literature is replete with mythological fables; that it seems necessary, in a work of this sort, to give some connected view of the subject, including a notice of such legends as are generally considered as descriptive of the leading events in the fabulous relations connected with the Avataras.

The word itself, in strictness, means advent, in which sense it is still retained in several dialects of India. But in its more extended signification, and in the sense now under consideration, it means an incarnation of a deity in the person generally of a human being; such incarnations have been innumerable. The three principal powers of the Deity, their consorts and offspring, the inferior deities, and **almost the whole host of mythological personages have had their Avataras, or descents on earth, for**

various purposes, of punishing tyrants and sinners, rewarding the good, or reclaiming the wicked.

When, however, speaking of the Avataras, it is generally meant to be confined to the ten incarnations of Vishnu, Dasavatara, as pre-eminently distinguishing them from others of a less important, or less potent nature.

These Avataras are usually thus arranged and named: 1. Matsya, or Fish, 2. Kurma, or Tortoise, 3. Varaha or Boar, 4. Narasingha, or Man-lion, 5. Vamana, or Dwarf, 6. Parasurama, 7. Rama, 8. Krishna, 9. Buddha, and 10. Kalki. Of these, nine are past, the tenth is yet to come.

When we hear that the Hindus speak of the Deity having been thus incarnated, we must understand it with some qualification; for, in fact, there is, perhaps, scarcely one point in their mythological religion that the whole race of Hindus have faith in. There are sectaries and schismatics without end who will believe only certain points that others abjure; individuals of those sects dissent from the doctrines believed by the majority; other philosophical sceptics will scarcely believe anything, in opposition to their easy-faithed brethren, who disbelieve nothing. Thus some Saivas, or followers of Siva, admit the sacredness of the Avataras of Vishnu, but in different degrees or potency and sanctity; they generally admit the personified interposition of the preserving attribute or the Deity in the affairs of the world, without yielding the point of supremacy in the prototype.

And some zealous Vaishnavas, or followers of Vishnu, giving themselves up to his adoration in some incarnation—Krishna, or Rama, for instance, reject with indignation, commensurate with their zeal or bigotry, all farther application of divine terms. Hence may, in part, be discerned the liability under which inquirers labour, of being misled by sectaries into receiving schism as orthodoxy and of forming general conclusions from individual or partial information. But, in fact, there is no general orthodoxy among Hindus, any more than among Christians; nor can it be expected: in the restlessness and diversity of men's minds such a thing is not in nature or reason. All religions profess alike belief in the Deity, and array him in nearly similar attributes; but when the idea of interposing incarnations be received, faith and reason are let loose in content, and it is admitted or rejected, or modified, according to the feelings, or unhappily, in many cases, according to the interests, or individuals.

Matsya, or Fish

This Avatara has been demonstrated to have immediate reference to the general deluge, and to be the same history disguised in oriental fiction of that event. Jones assents to the opinion of Bochart, that the fable of Saturn was raised on the true history of Noah:

he shows that the seventh Manu, Satyavrata corresponds in station and character. In his reign, the Hindus believe the whole earth to have been destroyed by a flood, including all mankind, who had become corrupt, except the pious prince himself, the seven Rishis, and their several wives; who, by command of Vishnu, entered a spacious vessel, accompanied by pairs of all animals.

Vishnu, assuming the form of a fish, commanded the ark to be fastened by a cable, formed of a vast serpent, to his stupendous horn, secured thereby until the flood subsided; when he and Brahma slew a monster named Hayagriva, who, while Brahma was reposing at the end of a Kalpa, stole the Vedas, and mankind had consequently fallen into the depths of ignorance and impiety. This mighty demon is called the prince of Danavas; his name means Horse-necked. The Vedas, having been recovered, the world was progressively repeopled with pious inhabitants, descendants of the devout Satyavrata and his favoured companions. The history of this Avatara is the subject of the first Purana, or sacred poem, consisting of 14,000 stanzas, and is concisely told in the eighth book of the Sri Bhagavata, or life of Krishna.

Kurma, or the Tortoise

The second grand Avatara of Vishnu, in the form of a tortoise, evidently refers also to the flood. In that of the Matsya, or Fish, we find the necessity of a deluge to cleanse the world from its sinful taints. By the demon Hayagriva

Matsya—the Fish Avatara

having stolen the Vedas while Brahma was dozing, we must understand the dereliction of mankind from the doctrines and conduct laid down in the scriptures, and the criminal indifference of their pastors. The preserving attribute of the Deity interposed, saved a remnant of creatures from destruction, and, by recovering the scriptures, reclaimed mankind to purity of faith and conduct.

For the purpose of restoring to man some of the comforts and conveniences that were lost in the flood, Vishnu is fabled to have become incarnate again in the form of a tortoise: in which shape he sustained the mountain Mandara, placed on his back to serve as an axis, whereon the gods and demons, the vast serpent Vasuki serving as a rope, churned the ocean for the recovery of the Amrita, or beverage of immortality. The history of this Avatara forms an episode in the Mahabharata.

The result of the operation that chiefly distinguished this Avatara was the obtainment of fourteen articles, usually called fourteen gems. These fourteen jewels are thus enumerated: 1. The Moon, Chandra, 2. Sri, or Lakshmi, the goddess of fortune and beauty, 3. Sura, wine; or Suradevi, the goddess of wine, 4. Ucchaisrava, an eight-headed horse, 5. Kaustubha, a jewel of inestimable value, 6. Parijata, a tree that spontaneously yielded everything desired, 7. Surabhi, a cow similarly bountiful, 8. Dhanwantari, a physician,

Kurma—the Tortoise Avatara

9. Airavat, the elephant of Indra, 10. Shankh, a shell conferring victory on whoever should sound it, 11. Dhanusha, an unerring bow, 12. Vish, poison, or drugs, 13. Rambha, the Apsara, a beautiful and amiable woman, and 14. Amrita, the beverage to immortality.

Varaha, or the Boar

In this Avatara Vishnu is generally represented four-handed, armed as usual, and with the head of a boar, on whose tusks rests a crescent, containing in its concavity an epitome of the earth, which had been immersed in the ocean as a punishment for its iniquities. So that this, as well as the two former Avataras, seems to be a repetition of the story of the deluge; the second combines with it a portion of astronomical allegory; and none of the other of the ten Avataras have any apparent reference to the universal catastrophe, so pointedly indicated by the first three, which are understood to have occurred in the earliest ages of Hindu history, if such a chaotic mass as their fabulous records may be dignified by such a term.

It is related in one fable, that a Daitya, named Hiranayakasipu, or the golden-eyed, passed a long life in practising religious austerities in honour of Brahma, and was requited by the appearance of the deity, with a promise of granting any boon he should ask. He required, as usual in these stories, to become universal monarch, and to be exempt from hurt by noxious animals, which he

Varaha—the Boar Avatara

enumerated, but omitted the hog. The ambitious Daitya, after obtaining his wishes, became excessively wicked and presumptuous; to such a degree as to seize on the earth, and carry it with him into the depths of the ocean. The interposition of the preserving power of the deity now became necessary, and Vishnu, assuming the form of a boar, a symbol of strength, dived into the abyss; and after a dreadful contest of a thousand years, slew the wicked monster, and restored the earth on the point of his tusks. Another legend says, that Vishnu emanated from Brahma's nostrils in the shape of a pig, and grew naturally to a boar.

Narasingha, or Man-lion

Two etherial warders of Vishnu's palace were cursed with banishment from his presence, for insolence to Sanaka, who, attended by the seven Rishis, was approaching to reverence the deity. Lakshmi was desirous of witnessing a battle, and Vishnu, to gratify her curiosity, willed this insolence on the part of his servants. The sentence of eternal exite was mitigated to seven transmigrations; during which, if they performed their duty of sincere Vaishnavas faithfully, their crime would be expiated: or, if they preferred to seven faithful transmigrations, three as Daityas, and enemies of Vishnu, taking consequences, they might be restored to Vaikuntha at the end of their third unholy lives. The latter, as was foreseen, they determined on, and first became the Daityas of the third and fourth Avataras; and

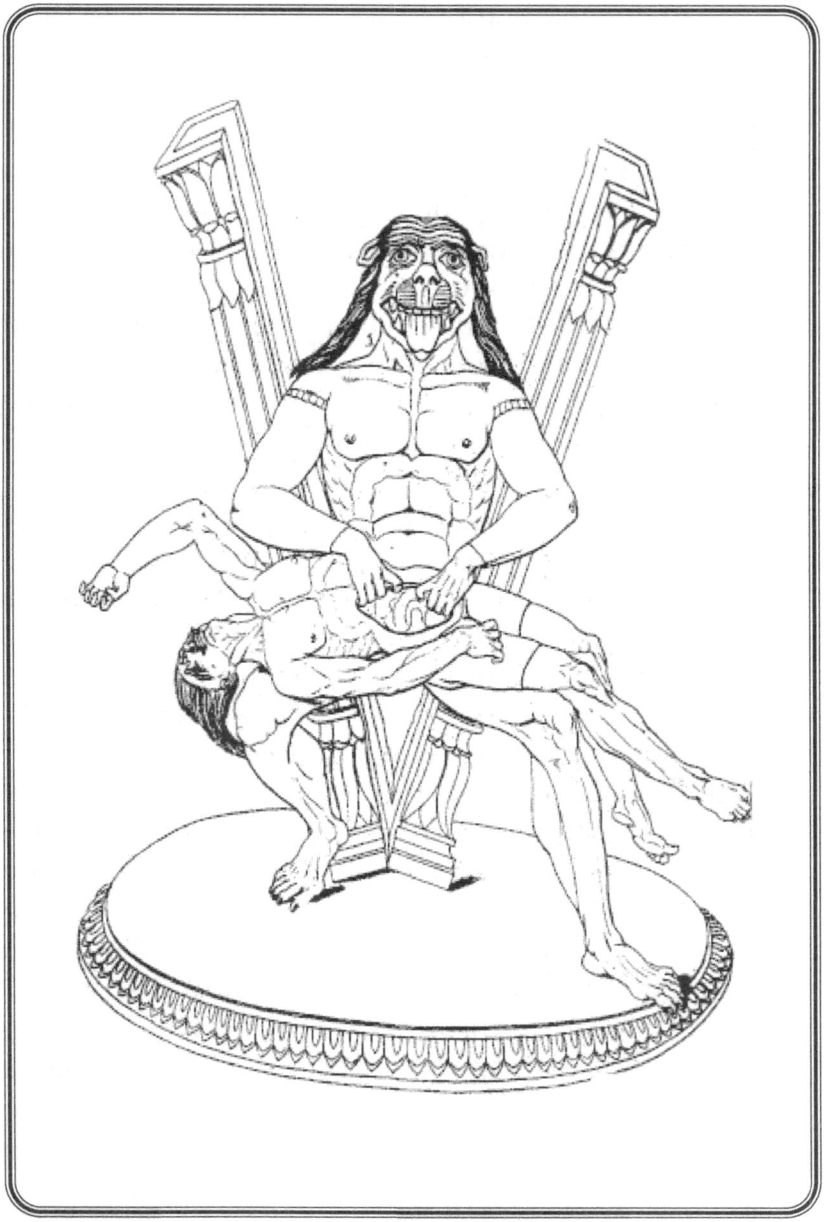

Narasingha—the Man-Lion Avatara

in the character of Hiranyakasipu, one of them was slain by Vishnu, incarnated for that purpose in the form of half-man and half-lion to account for which, the following legend is current.

The Daitya performed for ten thousand years the most rigorous austerities in honour of Brahma, and, as usual, obtained the boon he sought; which, in addition to universal monarchy, was an exemption from death by the means either of god or man, or of any animal; either by night or day; within doors, or without; on earth, or in heaven.

His arrogance now became so great, that his impiety was insufferable; and Vishnu proceeded to the farther gratification of his inquisitive consort, by exhibiting a conflict, short, but extremely fierce, in variation of that she had before been spectatress of, in the Varahavatara, which lasted, as related, a thousand years. He accordingly inspired the Daitya's virtuous son, Prahlada, to a commencement of a controversy with his impious father, involving the perplexing question of omnipresence, which is ingeniously enforced by the virtuous youth.

"Is then the deity here?" vociferated the father, pointing to a pillar that stood just on the threshold of the house; and on being answered affirmatively, he in blasphemous defiance smote the pillar with his sword. It was now evening; and the pillar rent asunder, exhibited the terrific spectacle of the deity in the monstrous shape of half-man, half-lion, Narasingha; who issuing forth, attacked Hiranyakasipu, and after a severe conflict of an hour, seized his devoted opponent by the hair, and at the moment when the day ends, dragged him to the severed pillar, and rent him into pieces.

Vamana, or the Dwarf

The four first Avataras are said to have occurred in the earliest, or Satya, age of the Hindus; corresponding in character with the golden or virtuous age of the fabulists of other regions. The fifth happened in the second, or Treta Yuga.

Bali, a monarch reasonably virtuous, was still so elated by his grandeur, that he omitted the essential ceremonies and offerings to the deities; and Vishnu finding it necessary to check the influence of such an example, resolved to mortify and punish the arrogant Raja. He therefore condescended to become the son of Kasyapa and Aditi, and the younger brother of Indra, and assumed the form of a wretched Brahmin dwarf; and appearing before the king, asked a boon, which being promised, he demanded as much as he could pace in three steps; nor would he desire farther, although urged by Bali to demand something more worthy of him to give.

The boon asked and yielded, was, as usual, the sovereignty of the universe, which includes the three regions of the earth, heaven, and hell.

Vishnu, on obtaining the king's promise, required a ratification of it; which is performed by pouring water on the hand of the applicant. This Bali proceeded to do, although warned of the consequences; for he scorned not to ratify that for which his royal word stood pledged.

As the water fell into his hand, the dwarf's form expanded till it filled the world; and Vishnu now manifesting himself, deprived Bali at two steps of heaven and earth, but, he being on the whole a virtuous monarch, left Patala, or Hell, still in his dominion. In this character Vishnu is sometimes called Trivikrama, the three-steptaker.

It is maintained by some Vaishnavas, that the ratifying stream, poured on the hand of Vishnu in this Avatara, was the river Ganga; which, falling from the hand of the miraculous dwarf, descended thence upon his, now Vishnu's, foot, whence, gushing as a mighty river, it was received on the head of Siva.

The pictures of this Avatara, of which I have many, usually represent Bali in the act of pouring the water into the dwarf's hand, through a spouted vessel. In some, the evil counsellor, Sakra, represented with one eye or holding his hand before the other; Sakra is, in fact, the same with Indra; and as Vrihaspati, is the counsellor or preceptor to the gods and Suras, so Sakra is adviser of the demons and Asuras, and is constantly employed in counteracting the divine beings and their endeavors for the good of man. To prevent the preserving power in this Avatara from accomplishing the projected end, in the punishment of pride and arrogance personified in Bali, Sakra apprised him of the deceit under which he was promising the universe away; but as the monarch had too much pride to recant his royal word, the evil counsellor assumed the form of a mosquito, and insinuating himself into the spout of the vessel, through which the ratifying stream was to pass, arrested its passage; when the dwarf, taking a straw to clear it, thrust out the eye of the gnat, a defect ever after retained by Sakra in all shapes; it is said to indicate the half-enlightenment of evil counsellors.

Kalki

This incarnation is yet to come. Vishnu, mounted on a white horse, with a drawn scimitar blazing like a comet, will, as minutely prophesied as to place, time, etc., end the present, or Kali age and renovate the creation with an era of purity.

The Hindus, like most other people, have thus a prophetic tradition of the coming of a punisher and redeemer. The Sybilline and Delphic oracles foretold it. The Chinese, Japanese, Siamese, and other eastern nations, have been taught to expect such an event; an idea that seems to prevail so generally among people so distinct, as to be deducible only from a common source.

The Three Ramas

Among the Avataras of Vishnu are recorded three favoured personages in whom the deity became incarnate, all named Rama. They are distinguished by the names of Balarama, usually called **Balaram, Parasurama** or Parasram, **and Ramachandra;** are all famed as great warriors, and as youths of perfect beauty.

The first named Balarama, was elder brother to Krishna, and greatly assisted him in his wars; so that, in this instance, Vishnu seems to have duplicated himself; for Parasurama, and Ramachandra, were cotemporaries.

Of Parasurama it is related that he was born near Agra, in the Treta Yuga or second age. His parents were Jamadagni, whose name appears as one of the Rishis, and Renuka. Jamadagni, in his pious retirement, was entrusted by Indra with the charge of the wonderful boon-granting cow, Kamadhenu or Surabhi, and on one occasion, regaled the Raja who was on a hunting party, in so magnificent a manner, as to excite his astonishment, until he learned the secret of the inestimable animal possessed by his host. Impelled by avarice, or rather heart-hardened by the gods, who willed the Raja's punishment, should appear to be the immediate result of that base passion, the cow was demanded from the holy Brahmin; and on refusal, force and stratagem were employed, which ended in the death of Jamadagni, but without success as to the

Balarama

acquisition of the desired animal, which disappeared. Renuka became a Sati, that is, burnt herself with her husband's corpse, charging the Raja with the guilt of double murder, imprecating curses on his head, and enjoining their valorous son Rama to avenge the death of his parents by the condign punishment of the impious Raja, whose measure of iniquity and oppression was completed by this final atrocity.

The prayers or imprecations of a Sati are never inefficiently uttered; the great gods themselves cannot listen to them unmoved. Vishnu accordingly inspired Rama, who appears to have been previously educated by Mahadeva, on Kailasa, with a portion of his divinity, and sent him forth to combat the Raja; who, after twenty battles, was slain, the military race of Kshattriyas annihilated, and his usurped kingdoms were relieved from oppression.

The pictures of this Avatara generally represent the combat between Parasurama and the Raja with his twenty arms, some of which are scattered about, severed by the weapon of his semi-divine opponent. The miraculous cow, the immediate source of the contention, is sometimes seen taking her flight in the air.

After a life spent in mighty and holy deeds, Rama gave his whole property in alms, and retired to the Konkan—the low country between Sural and the southern cape,

Parasurama

although not the whole extent of this tract—where he is said to be still living.

The *Ramayana* contains the heroic description of the battles and life of all three Ramas, although it more particularly details the exploits of Ramachandra, so distinguished from his royal father, Dasaratha. The name of this heroic monarch means, whose car had borne him to ten regions; that is, to the eight cardinal and two intermediate points, the zenith, and nadir. He was a descendant from Surya, and one of his ancestors, the great Raghu, had conquered the seven dwipas, or the whole earth.

Since my plates, illustrative of this Avatara, were engraved, the first volume of a translation of the *Ramayana* has been published in Calcutta and London. I had prepared a long article, collected from the communications of Brahmins, comprising an abstract of the *Ramayana*, as far as it relates to the history and adventures of Dasaratha, his three wives, and their offspring; Rama's contest for, and acquisition of, Sita; her origin, seizure, and escape from Ravana; and many particulars of Hanuman, and other mythological persons. Some of these may be introduced incidentally in this work; but the publication of the Ramayana will give them in a form so much more full, authentic, and correct, that I shall altogether omit the article alluded to. The learned will now be able to estimate the assertion of Sir William Jones, that Valmiki's great epic poem, the *Ramayana*, in unity of

Ramachandra

action, magnificence of imagery, and elegance of diction, far surpasses the elaborate work of Nonnus, in forty-eight books, entitled *Dionysiaca;* and how far the heroes of the two poems, Rama and Dionysos, be the same.

Ramachandra is the favourite subject of heroic and amatory poetics; he is described "of ample shoulders; brawny arms, extending to the knee;. neck, shell-formed; chest, circular and full, with auspicious marks; body, hyacinthine; with eyes and lips of sanguine hue; the lord of the world; image of Vishnu himself; the source of joy to Ikshwaku's race. He is also called Raghava, or the descendant of Raghu; and Shyamala, or blue-bodied, an appellation of Krishna, as well as of the prototype of both—Vishnu. The epithet of Kaka-pakshadhara, or crow-winged, is given to Rama and to other warriors, from a certain mode of shaving the head, leaving the hair over the ears only, resembling wings as is fancied.

Sita is said to have been so named, from Set, a field, or furrow, she having been found in a field, apparently about five years old, enclosed in a box, by a Brahmin at plough; and was presented to the childless Raja Janaka, after whom she is called Janaki. Sita, however, means fair, or white, and may be thence derived—"Endued with youth, beauty, sweetness, goodness, and prudence; an inseparable attendant on her lord, as the light on the moon; the beloved spouse of Rama, dear as his own soul, formed by the illusion of the Deva, amiable, adorned with every charm," Sita is also a favourite in descriptive poetry, and is held forth as an example of conjugal affection. The name of Rama is used beyond the pale of his own sectarists, in supplication and praise. 'Ram-ram' is a usual salutation, like our Good Morrow, between friends at meeting or passing, and is used by both Vaishnavas and Saivas.

Krishna

In this Avatara Vishnu is said, by his sectaries to have **manifested himself in a degree of power and glory far exceeding any other of his forms;** in which he assumed only an *ansa*, or portion of his divinity, while Krishna was Vishnu himself in mortal mould. His mortal parents were Vasudeva (meaning the giver of wealth) and Devaki. In a picture I have the miraculous escape of the infant over the Yamuna is represented, conveyed by his father, and protected by Sesha, or immortality; the guards placed by Kansa over his pregnant sister having failed in their vigilance. Kansa, enraged, ordered all newly born infants to be slain; but Krishna escaped his various snares: one of which was sending a woman, named Putana, with a poisoned nipple, to nurse him. He was fostered by an honest herdsman, named Nanda, and his amiable wife, Yasoda, or the giver of honour; and passed the gay hours of youth, dancing, sporting, and piping, among a multitude of young Gopas, or cowherds, and Gopis, or milkmaids, from whom he selected nine as favourites.

I have many pictures and casts of him in the character of Murlidhar, piping to the damsels and herds of Govardhan.

At the age of seven he uplifted, on the tip of his little finger, the mountain Goverdhan, the Hindu Parnassus, to shelter the Gopa and Gopis from the wrath of Indra, who, enraged with jealousy at the diminution of his votaries and sacrifices, consequent to the adoration of Krishna, attempted to destroy them by a partial deluge. This story is related from the *Matsya Purana*, whence Sir W. Jones has thus poetically introduced it in his hymn to Indra. The bard

—"Smil'd, and, warbling in a softer mode,
Sang the red lightning, hail, and whelming rain
O'er Gokul green, and Vraja's nymph-lov'd plain,
By Indra hurl'd, whose altars ne'er had glow'd,
Since infant Krishna rued the rustic train—
Now thrill'd with terror. Them the heavenly child
Call'd, and with looks ambrosial smil'd:
Then, with one finger rear'd the vast Govardhan,
Beneath whose rocky burden,
On pastures dry, the maids and herdsmen trod:—
The lord of thunder felt a mightier god."

Krishna passed a life of a most extraordinary and incomprehensible nature,

Krishna, with Mother Devaki Sucking her Breast

His miracles are amazing, the legends are detailed with such prolixity in the modern poem, the *Sri Bhagavata,* which is esteemed as the eighteenth Purana. He is represented as the meekest, tenderest and most benevolent of beings, still, however, he fomented the terrible war described in the Mahabharat; he washed the feet of the Brahmins: he exhibited an appearance of excessive libertinism; but it was all Maya, or delusion; for he was pure and chaste in reality.

The comparison between Krishna and Apollo runs parallel in a great many instances. The destruction of Python by Apollo, the commentators tell us, means the purification of the atmosphere by the Bun from the mephitic exhalations consequent to the deluge; and Krishna's victory over the noxious Kaliya Naga, may, by those who, allegorising all poetical extravagance deprive poetry of half its beauties, be explained in the same manner. Like the Pythia serpent in the Apollo, Kaliya Naga enjoys also his apotheosis in those dedicated to the worship of Krishna. Apollo and Krishna are both inventors of the flute. One was disappointedly Daphne, who was turned formed into the Laurus, hence sacred to Apollo; Krishna's coy nymph was transformed into the Tulasi, alike sacred to him.

Krishna is seldom drawn in pictures unattended by females, and where seen with but one, she is always said to be Radha, his

Krishna and Radha, Dancing with Gopis

favourite mistress, or divine spouse. The number of his regular wives is said to be eight: 1. Rukmani, an incarnation of Lakshmi, 2. Yamunini, 3. Kalindi, a water nymph, daughter of the sun, 4. Satyabhama, 5. Lakshmani, 6. Mitravinda, 7. Satya, and 8. Vrinda. Besides these, he attached to him sixteen thousand women that he found virgins in the ample seraglio of a five-headed asura, who, for his manifold crimes, Krishna slew.

The legendary tales, descriptive of these events, are of great length and variety. Each of these sixteen thousand and eight women bore him ten sons, and each supposed herself the exclusive favourite of her lord.

In musical legends it is said, that there were, in the days of Krishna, sixteen thousand Ragas, or musical modes, or rather passions, or affections of the mind; and each of his Raginis, or musical nymphs, selected one of these Ragas, in which to modulate her strains for affecting and securing the heart of the amorous and harmonious deity. This may perhaps mean that Krishna, devoted to music, receives and enjoys every variety of modulation, multiplied to the number of 16,000, and fancifully personified in the form of nymphs, derived from the five-headed Asura—a five-stringed or five-stopped instrument.

Krishna's names are, like other deified personages, numerous. He being Vishnu, they enjoy several in common: Murari, Hari, Madhav (Vishnu destroyed the giant Madhu), Bhagavan, are among them.—Govinda, Gopala, Gokula, are derived from his occupation of herdsman.—Gopinatha, the Gopi's god.—Murlidhar, the Tuneful.—Kesu, Kesava, or Kesavi, refer to the fineness of his hair; Vanamali, to his pendent garland; Yadava, Varshneya, and Vasudeva, to his tribe and family.

The loves of Krishna and Radha, which, in the writings and conversation of the Hindus, are constantly adverted to, are said to mean, in their emblematical theology, the reciprocal attraction between the divine goodness and the human soul; and are told at large in the tenth book of the *Bhagavat*; and are the subject of the beautiful pastoral drama, entitled *Gita Govinda*, by Jayadeva, who wrote before our era.

The following tender lamentation of Radha, for the absence of her lord, I extract from this poem:

"Though he takes recreation in my absence, and smiles on all around him, yet my soul remembers him, whose languishing reed modulates an air, sweetened by the nectar of his quivering lips, while his ear sparkles with gems, and his eye darts amorous glances;—him, whose locks are decked with the plumes of peacocks, resplendent with many-coloured moons, and whose mantle gleams like a dark-blue cloud illumined with rainbows;—him, whose graceful smile gives new lustre to his lips, brilliant, and soft as a dewy leaf—sweet

and ruddy as the blossoms of Bandhujiva, while they tremble with eagerness to kiss the daughters of the herdsman;—him, who disperses the gloom with beams from the jewels which decorate his bosom, his wrists, and his ankles—him, on whose forehead shines a circlet of sandalwood, which makes even the moon contemptible, when it moves through irradiated clouds;—him, whose earrings are formed of entire gems, in the shape of the fish makara on the banners of love—even the yellow-robed god, whose attendants are the chief of deities, of holy men, and of demons;—him, who reclines under a gay Kadamba tree, who formerly delighted me while he gracefully moved in the dance, and all his soul sparkled in his eyes. My weak mind thus enumerates his qualities; and though offended, strives to banish his offence.

"What else can it do? It cannot part with its affection for Krishna, whose love is excited by other damsels, and who sports in the absence of Radha. Bring, O my sweet friend! that vanquisher of tbe demon Kesi, to sport with me, who am repairing to a secret bower; who look timidly on all sides, who meditate with amorous fancy on his divine transfiguration. Bring him, whose discourse was once composed of the sweetest words, to converse with me, who am bashful on his first approach, and express my thoughts with a smile sweet as honey. Bring him, who formerly slept on my bosom, to recline with me on a green bed

of leaves just gathered, while his lips shed dew, and my arms enfold him. Bring him, who has attained the perfection of skill in love's art, whose hand used to press these firm and delicate spheres, to play with me; whose voice rivals that of the Kokila and whose tresses are bound with waving blossoms. Bring him, who formerly drew me by the locks to his embrace, to repose with me; whose feet tinkle as they move with rings of gold and gems; whose loosened cone sounds as it falls, and whose limbs are as slender and flexible as the creeping plant."

"That god, whose cheeks are beautified by the nectar of his smiles, whose pipe drops in ecstasy from his hand, I saw in the grove encircled by damsels of Vraja; who gazed on him askance from the corner of their eyes. I saw him in the grove with happier damsels, yet the sight of him delighted me.

"Soft is the gale that blows over yon clear pool, and extends the clustering blossoms of the voluble Asoka; soft, yet grievous to me in the absence of the foe of Madhu. Delightful are the flowers of the Amra on the mountain top, while the murmuring bees pursue their voluptuous toil; delightful, yet afflicting to me, O friend! in the absence of the youthful Kesava."

The seemingly amorous conflicts of these ardent lovers are mere mystical descriptions of "the reciprocal attraction between the divine goodness and the human soul."—This is the emblematical theology of that Pythagoras admired and adopted; that of the Sufi poets,

Hafez, Sadi, and others among the Persians, and Solomon also, in his fine song, so beautifully inculcate.

Let us now turn to a work of a different description, and observe the terms in which Krishna is described in the *Bhagavat Gita*. It will not be easy to exceed them in sublimity, divesting them of their local and mythological allusions even in genuine theological language.

Arjun, the son of Pandu, addresses Krishna as "The Supreme Brahman: the most holy; the most high God; the Divine Being before all other gods; without birth; the mighty Lord; God of Gods; the universal Lord." In different parts of the Gita, he says of himself—" I am, of things transient, the beginning, the middle, and the end; the whole world was spread abroad by me in my invisible form. At the end of the period Kalpa, all things return into my primordial source; and, at the beginning of another Kalpa, all things create them all again.—I am the creator of mankind; uncreated, and without decay.—There is not anything greater than I; and all things hang on me, even as precious gems on a string.—I am the understanding of the wise, the glory of the proud, the strength of the strong; I am the eternal seed of all nature; I am the father and mother of this world, the grandsire, and the preserver; I am death and immortality; I am entity and non-entity; I am never-failing time; I am all-grasping death; and I am the resurrection."

"The great Brahman is my womb; in it I place my foetus; and from it is the production of all nature.—The great Brahman is the womb of all those various former beings which are conceived in every natural womb; and I am the father that soweth the seed.—I am the emblem of the immortal, and of the incorruptible; of the eternal, of justice, and of endless bliss.—Neither the Sun, nor the Moon, nor the Fire enlighteneth that place from whence there is no return; and which is the supreme mansion of my abode."

Sanjay, one of the interlocutors of the *Gita*, describes Krishna, as he revealed his "million forms divine" to Arjun: "Covered with every marvellous thing—the eternal God, whose countenance is turned on every side. The glory and amazing splendour of this mighty being may be likened to the Sun, rising at once into the heavens with a thousand times more than usual brightness.—The son of Pandu then beheld, within the body of the God of Gods, standing together, the whole universe divided forth into its vast variety."

Arjun, terrified at this wonderous exhibition, exclaims: "Thou art the Supreme Being! I see thee without beginning, without middle, and without end; of valour infinite; of arms innumerable; the Sun and Moon thy eyes; thy mouth a flaming fire; and the whole world shining with thy reflected glory. Having beholden thy dreadful teeth, and gazed on thy countenance, emblems of Time's last fire, I know not which way I turn; I find no peace.—Have mercy then, O God of Gods! thou mansion of the universe! and show me thy celestial form; with the diadem on thy head, and thy hands, armed with the club and chakra.—Assume then, O God of a thousand arms! image of the universe! thy four-armed form."

Mention is made of the festival of Holi, more classically called Holika; otherwise Phalgutsava, meaning the festival of Phalguna, it occurring in the month of that name, commencing about the full moon, at the approach of the vernal equinox. It is one of the greatest festivals among the Hindus, and almost all the sects seem to partake in its festivals and all ranks, from kings downward, appear animated by the season, which is peculiarly dedicated to Krishna. Images of the deity are carried about in *palkis*, and on elephants, horses, etc., attended by music and singing, and various antics.

Several other holidays, especially in honour of Krishna, occur: on one, gifts of water and gram, particularity of barley, with oblations of perfumes, and other religious rites, produce fruit without end in the next world. On another, the festival is called Ratha Yatra or the festival of the chariot, in which the images of Krishna and Balarama are borne about in a car by day; on this occasion Krishna is worshipped as Jagannatha, or lord of the universe. At the temple of that name in Orissa, the concourse of people is very great.

Krishna fought eighteen bloody battles with Deva-Kala-Yavana, in common language called **Deo-Kalyun, whence the Greeks easily made Deucalion.** He is represented in the Puranas as a most powerful prince, who lived in the western parts of India, and is called an incarnate demon, because he opposed Krishna, and was very near his ambitious projects; indeed Krishna was worsted in the seventeen first battles and was forced to have recourse to treachery, by which Kalyun was totally defeated in the eighteenth. The title of Deva is not of course given to Kalyun in the Puranas, but would probably have been given him by his descendants and followers.

Buddha

Such Hindus as admit Buddha to be an incarnation of Vishnu, agree in his being the last important appearance of the deity on earth; but many among the Brahmins, and other tribes, deny their identity; and the Buddhists do, in general, likewise assert the independent existence, and of course paramount character, of the deity of their exclusive worship. As most of Vishnu's Avataras were apparently destined for the accomplishment of some special object, so this of Buddha seems to have been for the purpose of reclaiming the Hindus from their proneness to animal sacrifice. The mild heresy preached by Buddha, a leading tenet of which is the sin of depriving any animal of life, would naturally alarm tile orthodox priesthood, whose coffers overflowed from the donations of affrighted sinners, and whose hierarchy was threatened by the dawn of reason and the diffusion of philosophy. It cannot therefore be supposed that such an innovation could be contemplated by the Brahmins without considerable jealousy.

In respect to the number of its followers, and the extent over which they have spread, the doctrines of Buddha have probably obtained greater dominion than those of any other religious persuasion. Although now comparatively trifling on the continent of hither India, **his doctrines are still retained, differing in externals, and divided into sects, throughout China and its tributary nations; in the great empires and states of Cochin China, Cambodia, Siam, Pegu, Assam, Tibet, Bhutan; many of the Tatar tribes;** and generally all parts east of the Ganges; including many of those vast and numerous islands in the seas eastward and southward of the farther Indian promontory, whose inhabitants have not been converted to Islamism. In these great and distant parts of the globe the tenets of Buddha, distinguished of count by various appellations, may be recognised as forming the religion of the people; an extent exceeding that either of the Mahomedan or Brahmanical religion, and outnumbering, perhaps, tbe followers of the religion of Jesus Christ.

Buddha Avatara

In a country civilised to a considerable degree of intellectual refinement where the imagination has room for expansion, and where the exuberance of writers is not chastened by criticism, or restrained by the dread of exposure through the press, every manuscript becomes equally a volume of historical record, yielding abundance of materials for the collating or inventive faculties of commentators. Hence, perhaps, the uncertainty of how or where the heresy or reformation of Buddha was introduced and promulgated; but most likely in a mild and temperate manner, operating chiefly by its reasonableness and humanity. We are told, and may perhaps occasionally witness, that the followers of Buddha are held in abhorrence by Brahmins and other zealous individuals of more orthodox sects; but, in fact, those sects and tribes, if we include them in the whole Brahmanical flock as opposed to the heresy of Buddha, are so numerous, and their tenets, although so different, so little understood or noticed by each other, that there seems no proof, or evidence, to conclude that the introduction or promulgation of this heresy was attended on its part with any violence.

A Saiva, or a Vaishnava, of another sect, becoming a Buddha, need not, I think, unless intemperately zealous, so far depart from his usual habits as to be an object of hatred or jealousy to his own sect or family. If but reasonably attached to his new faith—rather, perhaps, grafted on his old stock of beliefs, than eradicating it, he may endow his new type of the deity with the symbols that distinguished the objects of his former adoration: he may adorn it with the attribute of Surya, and worship Buddha and the Sun together; he may shadow him with Sesha, and recognise in Buddha half the mythological personages of his scarcely-rejected Pantheism.—In short in a rational and temperate spirit, and no convert is so likely to be mild and temperate as a Hindu, he may, I think, embrace all the advantages of this heresy without becoming an object of contempt with his own tribe or family, or materially departing from his polytheistic idolatry, or his superstitious practices.

In very ancient sculptures and excavations we find the image of Buddha among the other deities of Brahmanical beliefs. The cave on Dharapuri, called by us Elephanta, an island in Bombay harbour, is an instance of this; and this temple in itself may be called a complete Pantheon; for among the hundreds, I may, perhaps, say thousands, of figures there sculptured, every principal deity is found. Many deified heroes, in the more modern mythological romances, contained in some of the Puranas and Tantras, will have been exalted since the excavation of this wonderful cavern; but I strongly believe that all the gods of the Vedas, or, if I may so term them, all the legitimate Hindu deities, will be found in its different compartments—if not, indeed, too much defaced for recognition. In a little account, written and corrected by me in the cavern, I find the following noticed:—Brahma, Vishnu, Siva, Buddha, Ganesa, and Indra; and these are, in fact, all that are, by their forms or attributes, or vehiclcs, unequivocally distinguishable.

The figure of Buddha, in the temple of Dharapuri, is immediately on your left at entering, opposite to a similar compartment on the right, fifty-five feet distant, containing a spirited eight-armed colossal statue of Siva, in the act of drawing a sword. He is evidently, from his size and situation, a principal personage; yet not he to whom the temple seems peculiarly dedicated, which I apprehend to be the One Supreme Being.

In the magnificent excavations near Ellora, in the neighbourhood of Aurungabad, the image of Buddha is also seen, as well as the images of other deities; and although he is there likewise very respectably situated, he is not the paramount deity to whom the temples are in general dedicated. One, of a superb description that will presently be more particularly noticed, seems exclusively his, as are similar temples on Salsette, and near the village of Karle, between Bombay and Poona. Others on Salsette are said to exhibit Buddha as the paramount deity, as well also as the deities that may more immediately be nominated Brahmanical; at Amboly, for instance. But, although I have more than once visited this curious and singular excavation, the figures are so much injured by time, and, from the friable nature of the subterraneous rock, out of which it is dug, hastened so to decay, that I am not certain that I recognised other unequivocal Hindu deities; more accurate observers say they have.

Neither the grand cave, nor those inferior, at Kanheri, on Salsette, have, to the best of my recollection, any sculptures of the images of Brahmanical beliefs. May we be allowed, from these premises, to deduce a farther confirmation of the idea, that the Buddha incarnation of Vishnu, and the sectorial deity of that name, exclusively worshipped by so many different nations under different forms and designations, are one and the same person?—and that such exclusive worship, and its accompanying ceremonies and privations, is a heresy or reformation, or whatever it may be termed, of the more ancient Brahmanical religion? Among European, as well as Indian inquirers, this opinion will find the most numerous, but, like other majorities, not the most zealous, supporters.

The following is the memoranda made in the Elephanta cave, descriptive of tbe compartment containing Buddha:

"On the left, immediately entering the cave, is Buddha sitting on an expanded lotus; the stem of which is supported by two much-mutilated males. On Buddha's left is a well-executed plantain tree; the trunk, with several leaves, pretty perfect; over the tree is Garuda carrying Vishnu; Garuda's beak and face damaged; and two of Vishnu's arms broken off—in one of them he held a lotus: over Vishnu is a male figure, mounted in a spirited style on a quadruped of equivocal species; its hoofs are discernible, and it may be a horse. On Buddha's right, in the superior corner, is Brahma sitting on a lotus, on the calyx of which are three or four well-embossed swans. The remains of an animal, like a lion, may be traced near the males who hold the stem of the lotus supporting Buddha; several groups of figures, in bold relief, overspread him; some hold chowries: Buddha's head-dress is finely ornamented; several crescents are among its ornaments; and a large rose projects on each side, behind his head, as if confining his hair. If Buddha were standing, he would be about fifteen feet high: the whole compartment, or niche, is about eleven feet square; the niche is indented four feet into the rock.

• • •

5

Siva's Sons: Ganesa, Kartikeya, Virabhadra, Bhairava

Ganesa

Ganesa is the Hindu **god of prudence and policy; he is the reputed eldest son of Siva and Parvati,** and is represented with an elephant's head, an emblem of sagacity; and is frequently attended by a rat, sometimes riding on one, the conduct of that animal being esteemed by the Hindus as peculiarly marked by wisdom and foresight; he has generally four hands, but sometimes six, or eight, or only two. **He is invoked by a Hindu, I believe of all sects, in the outset of any business:** if he builds a house, an image of Ganesa is previously propitiated and set up on or near the spot; **if he writes a book, Ganesa is saluted at its commencement,** as he is also at the top of a letter; beginning a journey, Ganesa is implored to prote44ct him, and, for the accommodation of travellers, his image is occasionally seen on the roadside, especially where two roads cross; but sometimes it is little else than a stone, rudely chiselled into something like an elephant's head, with oil and red ochre daubed over it, decorated, perhaps, with a chaplet of flowers by some pious neighbour or traveller. It is common to see a figure of the god of prudence in or over bankers and other shops; and, on the whole, there is perhaps no deity in the Hindu Pantheon so often seen and addressed.

Ganesa has not always a mouse under him, near him, but is oftener seen without; fourteen images in metal, and many pictures of him alone, and in groups; and his rat or mouse appears in a very small proportion of them.

Although Ganesa be almost always considered, and called, the son of Mahadeva and Parvati, there is yet a legend in the Siva Purana of his origin, that would exclude his reputed father from any share in the honour of his existence; I will give the legend as briefly as I can, as it contains other points of mythological fable.

Ganesa is sometimes represented with but one tusk; to account for which it is related in the Purana, that he was formed of fair proportions by Parvati, from the excrementitious particles and impurities of her own body, at which Mahadeva was jealous and displeased. Ganesa was his mother's champion, vindicating her honour and rights on all occasions, even against the infringements of Vishnu and his mother's lord. On one occasion Vishnu and Ganesa fought, and the latter would have been victor but for the interposition of Siva, who cut off Ganesa's head.

Ganesa

Parvati was greatly displeased and distressed at this event, and proceeded in revenge to austerities that threatened to derange the destinies of the universe, from which nothing could divert her but the restoration of her son; which, on the earnest application of the congregated deities, Siva consented to. But the severed head could not be found; and it was determined to fix on his trunk the head of the first animal that should make its appearance, which happened to be an elephant with but one tooth. Siva adopted Ganesa; and all the deities, to appease and console Parvati, consented that he should on all occasions be first invoked,

Another legened states that, in a desperate combat, Ganesa, having exhausted all means of offence, plucked out one of his tusks, and hurled it at his adversary.

In a picture of mine, Ganesa is represented with two wives whose names were Siddhi and Buddhi, daughters of Vishwarupa; who were sought also by Ganesa's brother, Kartikeya; and it was agreed that whichever of them could first traverse the earth should win and have the damsels. Ganesa, in the disputation, proved, by his logical talents and aptness at quotation of divine texts, that he had so done, and obtained the prize long before his brother's return from his weary pilgrimage; to the great disquiet of both families, when the sophistry of Ganesa was exposed.

Under the head of Sects is an account of the five grand divisions of Hindus who exclusively worship a single divinity and one of these divinities is Ganesa, and the sectaries who thus worship him are called Ganapatyas.

His Highness the Peshwa has a very magnificent room in his palace at Poona, called the Ganesa Room, in which, on particular festivals in honour of Ganesa, he receives numerous visitors; I have seen more than a hundred dancing girls in it at one time. At one end, in a recess, is a fine gilt figure, I believe, in marble of this deity, and many other mythological decorations amount.

Images and pictures of Ganesa are very common.

Kartikeya

Kartikeya, brother of Ganesa, his six faces. In the *Ramayana*, the origin of Kartikeya, is detailed: the great mountain Haimavat, sovereign of mountains, had two daughters, of unparalleled beauty, by his spouse Mera, daughter of Meru. Their names were Ganga and Uma; the former was yielded in marriage to all the celestials at their earnest solicitation. Uma remained a virgin, and became a devotee of extraordinary rigidity; but was at length espoused by the incomparable Rudra, who devoted himself to connubial enjoyment, but without any issue. All the gods, to whom the production of a son was of great moment, addressed Hutashana (Agni), saying, "Accompanied by Vayu, combine thyself with the Rudrian energy; which being poured forth, was pervaded by Agni, for the purpose of producing the puissant Kartikeya, resplendent as the god of fire himself. Uma enraged at this promised offspring, in which she was not participant, laid her maledictions on all the celestials for soliciting such a solitary production, and on the earth for receiving it.—"Never," she imprecated, "may ye obtain offspring from your own spouses, since ye have debarred me, desirous of offspring, from nuptial rites." This curse Rudra declared to be irrevocable, but promised that a son should, by the influence of Agni, be produced by Ganga; which son would be acknowledged by Uma, her younger sister, Ganga, receiving the influence of Agni, thus addressed him who precedes all the celestials—"O divine one! filled with inexpressible pain, I am unable to bear thy influence; I am burning by this fire." He, who consumes the oblations made to all the gods, Agni, or Fire, replied: "O sinless one! deposit thy burden here, on the side of Haimavat;" and she produced Kurara from her side.

The gods, with Indra and the Maruts, now delivered this son to the six Krittikas (the Pleiades), to be nourished by them; and they offering their breasts, the six-headed was nurtured, and named Kartikeya, the descendant of the Krittikas.

He is, notwithstanding, generally esteemed the second son of Siva and Parvati, the god

Kartikeya

of war, and commander of the celestial armies.

Subramani is another name for the subject of this article, used both on the Bombay and the Madras side of India, especially the latter. Sonnerat relates a Karnatic legend of his having sprang from Siva's central eye, to destroy the giant Souraparpma, whom he cut in two, and the severed monster assumed the shapes of a peacock and a cock; the former of which the victor determined to use as a vehicle, and the latter to be borne in his standard.

We may suppose that the number six is often found appertaining to this six-headed, six-armed, six-mouthed, personage. The sixth day, severally, of the months Margasirsha and Chaitra, are sacred to the god of arms and war.

Virabhadra

Virabhadra, a heroic persona, now demands our notice; he is sometimes called a son, sometimes an Avatara, of Siva. He is represented with the attributes of his prototype, the Linga and Nandi, and armed with bow and arrow, sword and shield. It is related in the *Ramayana* that the famous bow of Vishnu was used by Siva with great effect at the destruction of Daksha's sacrifice.

Virabhadra is a personage of extensive celebrity, and his exploits are recorded in ancient and sacred books. Sonnerat mentions

Virabhadra

him in the Karnatic under the name of Virapatrin, as the fourth son of Siva, produced with a thousand heads and a thousand arms by the sweat of his body to avert the effects of a sacrifice. In the *Siva Purana* it is mentioned, that he was produced from a drop of Siva's sweat.

Bhairava

Bhairava is another of Siva's sons; sometimes, like Virabhadra, spoken of as an Avatara: the name being derived from Bheru, meaning terrific, tremendous, etc., is, as has been before said, applied also to Siva, his spouse, and their offspring.

It is, I believe, chiefly among the Marathas that this form of Siva is worshipped; with them it is called Bheroba; and his spouse is named Yugasiri, pronounced Jogasery. Their images are met with more commonly than that of any other deity; of different discretions, separately and together, I have, imagine, nearly a hundred in copper and brass; with an appearance of having been buried.

In one of them Bhairava is four-handed, holding the commonest attributes of Vishnu, the Sankh and Chakra; while most of the other distinctions appertain to Siva, the cup, linga, and bull, especially. The ram's or goat's head refers, I conjecture, to Daksha's substitute; for some legends attribute the decapitation of Brahma in that form to Bhairava; the horse, five balls, sun, moon, are very commonly seen with this and with other characters.

Bhairava

Sonnerat notices this deity as honoured in the Karnatak: he calls him Vairevert, third son of Siva; produced from his breath to humble the arrogance of Brahma, one of whose heads he wrenched off, and used the skull to receive the blood of his other antagonists.

• • •

6

Narayana, Manus, Apsaras

Narayana

With the early investigators of Hindu mythology the character of Narayana must have been the source of considerable embarrassment; nor is it yet entirely cleared from contradiction and obscurity; the latter, perhaps, necessarily attendant on a subject so little within the scope of research, and on which contradictory information will be given according to the religious opinions or sect of the informant.

If inquiry be made of a Vaishnava, or one of the exclusive adorers of Vishnu, he will not fail of exalting the object of his own adoration to the throne of the One only Almighty Being; and with that view will call him Narayana, although in fact such name is not strictly applicable to that Being, but to his Spirit, if such a personification can be conceived. The Gokulastyas, a branch of the Vaishnavas, will similarly exalt Krishna, the exclusive object of their adoration; and in other passages we are scarcely able to distinguish the persons of Narayana and Brahma. It is only, therefore, from their own books that, in this instance particularly, any authentic information can be obtained of the Hindu doctrines; and even then, we must keep in mind the probable sectorial bias of both compiler and commentator.

Sir William Jones has addressed a hymn to this deity, and in the argument prefixed, says, "A complete introduction to it would be no less than a full comment on the Vedas and Puranas of the Hindus, but this is not the place for so vast a disquisition. It will be sufficient here to notice, that the inextricable difficulties attending the notion of material substances, coucernmg which

"We know this only, that we nothing know;"

induced many of the wisest among the ancients, and some of the most intelligent among the moderns, to believe that the whole creation was rather an energy than a work, by which the infinite Being, who is present at all times in all places, exhibits to the minds of his creatures a set of perceptions like a wonderful picture, or piece of music, always varied, yet always uniform; so that all bodies and their qualities exist, indeed, to every wise and useful purpose, but exist only as they are perceived: a theory no less pious than sublime, and as different from any principle of atheism as the brightest sunshine differs from the blackest night. This illusive operation of the

Narayana, with Lakshmi in his Lap

Deity the Hindu philosophers call Maya, or Deceplion."

In the first stanza of the hymn are represented the sublimest attributes of the Supreme Being, and the three forms in which they most clearly appear to us—Power, Wisdom, and Goodness. The second stanza comprises the doctrines of the Divine Essence, and archetypal ideas, The third and fourth are taken from the Book of Manu, and the eighteenth Purana, entitled *Sri Bhagavat*. From Brahman, or the Great Being, in the neuter gender, is formed Brahma, in the masculine; and the second word is appropriated to the creative power of the Divinity.

The Spirit of God, called Narayana, or moving on the water, has a multiplicity of other epithets in Sanskrit; the principal of which are introduced expressly, or by allusion, in the fifth stanza of the hymn. The sixth ascribes the perception of secondary qualities by our senses to the immediate influence of Maya; and the seventh imputes to her operations the primary qualities of extension and solidity.

"Hail, self-exlstent, in celestial speech,
Narayana from thy wat'ry cradle nam'd.—
Or Venamali;
Or high Pritamesh"

According to Manu, "The waters are called Nara, because they were the first production of Nara, or the Spirit of God; and since they were his first *ayana*, or place of motion, he is thence named Narayana, or moving on the waters."

It is commonly understood, in the pictures where Brahma is seen seated on lotus issuing from the navel of a figure recumbent on a vast many-headed serpent, that such figure is Vishnu; but he ought, perhaps, as has been before stated, to be rather considered as Narayana, or Vishnu under that name, given him by the Vaishnavas.

Images of Mahadeva-Parvati are seen so much in form and posture like those of Lakshmi-Narayana, as not to be known one from the other but from their distinguishing attributes. In the caves at Ellora, he is sitting in a graceful attitude in the lap of Mahadeva; he has one of his four hands on her breast, and another similarly placed on an attendant female; in this instance, were it not for the peculiar style in which Mahadeva's hair is bound up, the subject might be mistaken for Lakshmi-Narayana. Parvati is, however, of a size proportional to Mahadeva.

In a profound and spirited hymn to Narayana, that deity, a personification of the Spirit of Brahman, as "he heavenly pensive on the lotus lay" said to Brahma, "Go; bid all worlds exist!" and the lotus is thus apostrophized.

> *"Hail, primal blossom! hail, empyreal gem!*
> *Kamal, or Padma, or whate'er high name*
> *Delight thee; say, what four-formed Godhead came,*
> *With graceful stole, and beamy diadem,*
> *Forth from thy verdant stem?—*
> *Full-gifted Brahma."*

But Brahma himself is sometimes considered as Narayana. The 30th and 31st chapters of the White, Yajur Veda are "related to the Purushamedha, a type of the allegorical immolation of Narayana, or of Brahman in that character."—And in a note alluding to the fabulous origin of the Vedas, a commentator is said to have had "recourse to the renovations of the universe. In one kalpa the Vedas proceeded from fire, air, and the sun; in another from Brahman at his allegorical immolation." Again "the allegorical immolation of Narayana" occurs and the epithet Narayana Purusha is given.

The Purushamedha means the sacrifice or immolation of Purusha. "Purusha means the primeval man, or primeval person." The hymn, called Purusha, recited among the ceremonies of the Sraddha, or oblations in honour of deceased ancestors, and followed by the music of flagelets, lutes, etc.

"The embodied spirit which hath a thousand heads, a thousand ears, a thousand feet, stands in the human breast, while he totally pervades the earth.

"That being is this universe, and all that has been, or will be; he is that which grows by nourishment; and he is the distributor of immortality.

"Such is his greatness; and therefore is he the most excellent embodied spirit; the elements of the universe are one portion of

him; and three portions of him are immortality in heaven.

"That threefold being rose above this world; and the single portion of him that remained in this universe, which consists of what does, and what does not, taste the reward of good and bad actions: again he pervaded the universe.

"From him sprung Viraj, from whom the first man was produced; and he, being successively reproduced, peopled the earth.

"From that single portion, surnamed the universal sacrifice, was the holy oblation of butter and curds produced; and this did frame all cattle, wild or domestic, which are governed by instinct.

"From that universal sacrifice were produced the strains of the Saman: from him the sacred meters sprung: from him did the Yajush proceed.

"From him were produced horses, and all beasts that have two rows of teeth: from him sprung cows, goats, and sheep.

"Him the gods, the demigods named Sadhya, and the holy sages, immolated as a victim on sacred grass; and thus performed a solemn act of religion.

"Into how many portions did they divide this being whom they immolated? What did his mouth become? What are his arms, his thighs, and his feet, now called?

"His mouth became a priest: his arm was made a soldier; his thigh was transformed into

a husbandman; from his feet sprung the servile man.

"The moon was produced from his mind; the sun sprung from his eye; air and breath proceeded from his ear; and fire rose from his mouth.

"The subtle element was produced from his navel; the sky from his head; the earth from his feet; and space from his ear. Thus did he frame worlds.

"In that solemn sacrifice which the gods performed with him as a victim, spring was the butter, summer the fuel, and sultry weather the oblation.

"Seven were the moats surrounding the altar; thrice seven were the logs of holy fuel at that sacrifice which the gods performed, immolating this being as the victim.

"By that sacrifice the gods worshipped this victim; such were primeval duties; and thus did they attain heaven, where former gods and mighty demigods abide."

Brahma seems, especially in the 11th verse, to be spoken of in the hymn, which, or the ceremony of Pururshamedha as before quoted, is stated by Mr. Colebrooke to "be a type of the allegorical immolation of Narayana, or Brahma in that character." Brahma and Narayana are in this instance identified; and from the circumstance of having Lakshmi as his wife, and bearing the attrihutes of Vishnu, as above described, Narayana is also unequivocally identified with the preserving power. Krishna, indeed, calls himself Narayana; at least is made to do so by Jayadeva, the spirited author of tbe *Gita Govinda*. In one Of Krishna's tender songs, addressed to his delightful mistress, the following is the burden.—"Give short raptures, sweet Radha! to Narayana thy adorer."

The *Siva Purana* contains a theogonical narrative, grounded of course on the doctrines or the Saivas, that includes various points of mythology, although not, perhaps, materially clearing the subject of its difficulties and contradictions. Here follows a brief abstract of it:

Brahman willing the creation of the world, produced two beings, male and female, Purusha and Prakriti: the latter with eight arms, most beautiful. They were subsequently called Narayana and Narayani; and from the benignity of Narayana proceeded the five elements—earth, air, water, fire, and ether, akas. From his navel, when reposing, issued a lotus, bearing Brahma; and from her sprung Vishnu: a quarrel ensued; and a third deity, the Linga, appeared, and appeased the creative and conservative powers, who respectively, assuming the form of a goose and a boar, sought in vain the source and end of Brahma, who in this Purana is of course identified with Siva. It proceeds to state how a Sakti sprang from Narayana, named Savitri (the Sun), whom Brahma espoused; and two others, Lakshmi and Parvati, who were taken to wife by Vishnu and Siva. How another form similar to Siva's sprang from a wrinkle in Brahma's forehead, and was named Rudra, and was in all respects the same as Siva; and also the same as both Brahma and Vishnu. The only distinction between tbe four was, that three proceeded from Prakriti, but himself, Siva, did not.

Of the Black Yajurveda a considerable portion, comprising an Upanishad, is called Narayana; or, to distinguish it from another Upanished of the Atharva, likewise so called, it is styled Maha Narayana, or Vrihan Narayana; that is, the Great Narayana.

A passage in the *Hitopadesa* speaks of Narayana as Brahman, comprehending in himself the three great powers —"The great and mighty Lord, Narayana; the author of Creation, Preservation, and Destruction; he will wipe away our sorrows."—On which, the learned translator Wilkins has this note—"Destruction: though this attribute more particularly belongs to Siva, yet it is common to allow the same powers to each of the three persons of the Hindu Trinity, Brahma, Vishnu (or Narayana,) and Siva, seeing they mean but one God—Brahman, or Brahma."

It would appear from this passage, that the author of the *Hitopadesa* was a Vaishnava, as, indeed, his name, Vishnu Sarma, indicates.

The *Ramayana* being the production of a Vaishnava, we may of course expect there to find Vishnu and Narayana identified.—

"Brahma, the sovereign of the gods: Sthanu," (a name of Siva) "and Narayana, chief of beings...Narayana, the all pervading"; "the imperishable Vishnu."

The Manus

Frequent mention is made in all Hindu writings and conversations, whether historical, scientific, or poetical, of certain mythological persons under the above designation; and in view to a ready reference to some general information respecting such beings, I shall here take the opportunity of introducing them to the reader's notice, explaining briefly, and as clearly as I am able, who they were.

It is said, in the Book of Manu, that the Mighty Power, having divided his own substance, became male and female; and from that female produced Viraj. Viraj produced the first Manu, named Swayambhuva; he, the ten Brahmadikas, or Prajapatis, whom he calls ten lords of created beings. They produced seven other Manus, whose names were Swayambhuva, Swarochesha, Uttama, Tamasa, Raivata, Chakshusha, and Satyavrata. These Manus are, by some authorities, said to have produced the seven Rishis; but others state the seven Rishis to have sprang immediately from Brahma: their names are Kasyapa, Atri, Vasistha, Viswamitra, Gautama, Jamadagni, and Bharadwaja.

It may be expedient to give a farther account of Viraj, as translated by Mr. Colebrooke, from the White Yajurveda:

"He, (the primeval being) felt not delight; therefore man delights not when alone. He wished the existence of another; and instantly he became such, as is man and woman in mutual embrace. He caused this, his own self, to fall in twain; and thus became husband and wife; therefore, was this body so separated as it were an imperfect moiety of himself. This blank, therefore, is completed by woman: he approached her, and thence were human beings produced.

"She reflected, doubtingly, 'How can he, having produced me from himself, incestuously approach me? I will now assume a disguise.' She became a cow, and the other became a bull, and approached her; and the issue were kine. She was changed into a mare, and he into a stallion; one was turned into a female ass, and the other into a male one; thus did he again approach her; and the one-hoofed kind was the offspring. She became a female goat, and he a male one; she was an ewe, and he a ram: thus he approached her; and goats and sheep were the progeny. In this manner did he create every existing pair whatsoever, even to the ants and minutest insect."

Mr. Colebrooke says: "The notion of Viraj dividing his own substance into male and female occurs in more than one Purana; so does that of an incestous marriage and intercourse of the first Manu and his daughter Satarupa; and the commentators on the

Upanishad understand that legend to be alluded to in this place. But the Institutes ascribed to Manu, make Viraj to be the issue of such a separation of persons, and Manu himself to be the offspring."

Ten Brahmadikas have been noticed and named; but the Puranas do not agree as to their number. There are but nine noticed in other passages of the Puranas: in the *Skanda Purana* it is declared that there were no more than seven; nor are authorities wanting to reduce them to three: namely, the three sons of Swayambhuva who was Brahma himself in a human shape.

Mr. Wilford thinks it likely that the seven Manus, the seven Brahmadikas, and the seven Rishis, to be the same, and to make only seven individual persons; first called Brahmadikas, children of Brahma, and created for the purpose of supplying the world with inhabitants. Having fulfilled this mission, they became sovereigns, or Manus; who, when far advanced in years, wlthdrew from the world to solitary places to prepare for death, and became Rishis, who, by their salutary counsels, and the example of their austerities, discovered the paths of virtue and rectitude to mankind.

But there is still much confusion in their persons and characters. It is, indeed, the first and last only that are usually heard of, the first, named Swayambhuva, or son of the Self Existent, is he who is supposed to have revealed the laws, known by the title of Manus; and that, in the time of the seventh Manu, surnamed Satyavrata, (called also Vaivaswata, or child of the Sun) the general deluge occurred. The first Sir William Jones judged to be the same with Adam; the other Noah, "the great progenitor and restorer of our species."

It may, perhaps, tend to give a clearer idea of these personages, if their names were placed together; they are here recapitulated:

Brahmadikas, or Prajapatis; that is, lords of prajas, or creatures	Manus	Rishis
Marichi	Swayambhuva	Kasyapa
Atri	Swarochasa	Atri
Angiras	Uttama	Vasishta
Pulastya	Tamasa	Viswamitra
Pulaha	Raivata	Gautama
Kritu	Chakshusha	Jamadagni
Vasishta	Satvavrata	Bharadwaja

In these lists we find the names of Atri and Vasishta both as Brahmanas and Rishis, but no other name is common to any two lists.

The Rishis have had the honour of becoming the seven bright stars in the great bear; and they are fabled to be married to the Pleiades. There being now but six of the latter, farther fables became necessary to reconcile the difference.

Near Vasishta (who is in lat. 60°N.) is a small star, representing his wife Arundhati.

Astrologers watch carefully their motions, because their influences are variously modified; and whatever new-married couples see them in an auspicious conjunction or position, they are surely to live happy together for a hundred years.

Before I notice an article of scandal respecting these brilliant ladies, I will mention that other legends speak favourably of Madam Anasuya, spouse of Atri, and of Ahilya, wife of Gotama; but, from being in bad company, their characters have suffered.

It is related that Agni, the ardent deity of Fire, was charitably disposed to communicate a portion of his warmth to these ladies; and situated as they were in the Arctic circle, we cannot much wonder at their complacency to such a comfortable suitor. But it is said that, he had not complete success; for that his wife (I suppose Swaha) dreading the resentment of the holy Rishis, successively assumed the shape and countenance of each of their desirable wives, and thus personifying them, satisfied her husband's ardour.

Arundhati, however, having always been exemplary as to holiness and sanctity, was not suspected on this unlucky occasion; but the other six Rishis, in consequence of scandalous reports, not only dismissed their sparkling spouses but, like great bears, drove them out of the Arctic circle; and they now shine the Pleiades. It would appear that they had qualified themselves for wet nurses, and accordingly nursed young Kartikeya; or were entrusted with his education, and were placed by him in the Zodiac.

The Pleiades, according to mythologists in the West, were entrusted likewise with the education of Bacchus, (who, according to Macrobius, was the same with Mars, or Kartikeya) and on that account he transported them into heaven. According to those writers, they suffered a real bodily pollution; and the seventh left her sisters and fled to the regions of the heavens within the Arctic circle: and this is the Arundhati of the Hindus.

Brahma is sometimes said to be Swayambhu, or the Self Existent, or the Supreme Being. Sometimes Brahma is called Swayambhuva, or son of the Self Existent, the name of the first Manu, who by some accounts is made Brahma's son, by others his grandson. By the Saivas Swayambhu is identified with Siva.

Of the five Manus who succeeded him I have seen little more than the names; the Hindu writings are very diffuse on the life and posterity of the seventh Manu, surnamed Vaivaswata, or child of the Sun. He is supposed to have had ten sons, of whom the eldest was Ikshwaku; and to have been accompanied by seven Rishis, an account of which explains the opening of the 4th chapter of the *Gita*. "This immutable system of devotion," says Krishna, "I revealed to Vivaswat, or the Sun, Vivaswat declared it to his son Manu; explained it to Ikshwaku: thus the chief Rishis know this sublime doctrine, delivered from one to another."

From this seventh Manu the whole race of men is believed to have descended; for the seven Rishis. who were preserved with him in the ark, are not mentioned as fathers of human families. But since his daugthter Ila was married to the first Budha, or Mercury, the son of Chandra, or the Moon, a male deity, whose father was Atri, son of Brahma (an allegory purely astronomical, or poetical) his posterity is divided into two great branches, called the Children of the Sun, from his own supposed father, and the Children of the Moon, from the parent of his daughter's husband.

Sir William Jones states Vivaswata to be the son of Surya, the son Kasyapa, or Uranus, the son of Marichi, or Light, the son of Brahma.

The reader will begin to be aware of the endless diversity of theogonical legends; or of those referring to the early animated productions of the different Hindu deities. One taken from the work of Anquetil Duperron, called by him *Oupnekhat*, or Upanishad* may be introduced in this place and, If not illustrating them, exhibiting at least another instance of their wildness, and perhaps inconsistency.

---

*Upnishad: the very first translation made into Latin by Duperron, of the sixty Upanishads published in Persian by Dara Shikoh, which drew the famous French philosopher Schopenhauer's attention and made them popular in the West.—Edlitor

Brahman said, "Rise up. O Rudra! and form man to govern the world."

Rudra immediately obeyed; he began the work; but the men he made were fiercer than tigers, having nothing but the destructive quality in their composition; and they soon destroyed one another, for anger was their only passion. Brahma, Vishnu, and Rudra, then joined their different powers, and created ten men, whose names were Narada, Daksha, Vasishta, Bhrigu, Kritu, Pulaha, Pulastya, Angira, Atri, and Marichi; (that is> Reason, Ingenuity, Emulation, Humility, Piety, Pride, Patience, Charity, Deceit and Morality) the general, name of whom is the Munis. Brahma then produced Dharma, Justice, from his breast; Adharma, Injustice, from his back; Labha, Appetite, or Passion, from his lips; and Kama, Love, or Desire, from his heart. The last was a beautiful female, and Brahma looked upon her with amorous emotions; but the Munis telling him she was his own daughter, he shrunk back, and Lajja, Shame, a blushing virgin, sprung from him; Brahma, deeming his body defiled by its emotions towards Kama, purified himself and partially changing it into ten females, who were respectively espoused by the Munis.

This may serve as a further specimen of the endless allegories in which the poetical fabulists have veiled the moral, scientific, and theological knowledge of the Hindus all of which, as well as history, and even arts, if not buried in, are obscured by, and intimately connected with their wild and bold mythology. Thus, again the Mahabharat is a continued allegory between man's virtues and his vices: the former personified under the names of the five sons of Pandu; of whom Bhima, Yudhishth-Ira, and Arjun, said to represent Justice, Fortitude, and Prudence, were by one mother, Kunti; two, Nakul and Sahadeva, personifications of Temperance and Wisdom, by Madri.

Man's manifold vices are personated by the hundred sons of Kuru, the brother of Pandu; hence a near relationship exists between Vice and Virtue.

I will here introduce other texts from the *Book of Manu*, with the like view of recording and giving some explanation of names of common occurrence.

"The eleven Rudras; the twelve Adityas; the eight Vasus; the Maruts, or genii of the winds; and the seven great Rishis, have performed this lunar penance as a security from all evil."

The names of the eleven Rudras I do not know nor their occupations, nor the reason of their peculiar number; they are distinctions of Siva in his character of Fate, or Destiny. Sankara is one, and the principal of them; and that name also appertains to other characters; Siva himself is sometimes so called.

The twelve Adityas are said to be the offspring of Aditi, the mother of the gods. They are emblems of the sun for each month of the year; and are themselves called Suns: their names are Varuna, Surya, Vedanga, Bhanu, Indra, Ravi, Gabhasti, Yama, Swarnareta, Divakara, Mitra, and Vishnu. Of these Vishnu seems to be considered as the first; for Krishna, describing his own pre-eminence, says, "Among the Adilyas, I am Vishnu."

A Vasu is one of the eight divinities who form a Gana, or assemblage of gods; and there are nine of those Ganas, of which nine Ganas or companies of deities, are enumerated in the *Amarkosh*. Ganesa is said to derive his name (Gan-Isa, Lord of the Ganas) from his supposed situation as the principal or president of those assemblages; although Agni, the god of Fire, is generally deemed the chief of the Vasus, eight of whom were among the earliest productions of Brahma.

The Maruts, or genii of the winds, have Pavan as their chief deity; of whom we shall take further notice when speaking of his son Hanuman. Marichi is also ranked as a chief among the Maruts.

"The Pitris, or great progenitors, are free from wrath; intent on purity; ever exempt from sexual passions; endued with exalted qualities: they are primeval deities who have laid arms aside."

Many tribes of Pitris are enumerated in the following texts:

"From the Rishis come the Pitris, or patriarchs; from the Pitris both Devas and

Danavas; from the Devas this whole world of animals and vegetables in due order."

The following text, introduces them to us in another character:

"A month of mortals is a day and a night of the Pitris, or patriarchs, inhabiting the Moon: the half, beginning with the full moon, is their day for action; and that, beginning from the new moon, is their night for slumber."

The time most peculiarly sacred to the names of the Pitris is the dark half of each month; the day of conjunction is the fittest day.

Yama is the sovereign of the Pitris.

The title Deva is very comprehensive, meaning generally a deity; Devi is its feminine; Devata is the plural of Deva.

Danava is the plural of Danu, the individual whence proceeded this race of evil spirits, of fallen angels. Asura means nearly the same, generally as Danava, although there may be different legendary accounts of their origin. Daitya and Rakshas are names of evil beings—spirits in other worlds or malignantly incarnate in this.

There are also good angels, Suras. These words, Sura and Asura, in the Hindu writings abound in allusions to their state of continued warfare. The terms Devarshi, Rajarshi. Maharshi, are nearly synonymous with Rishi, meaning saint, deified saint, great saint, or great sage. There are differences doubtless;

for Narada is reckoned the chief of the Devarshis, and appears among the Brahmadikas—as a Rishi. Krishna speaks of his "holy servants, the Brahmins and the Rajarshis" and says, "I am Bhrigu among the Maharshis" "and of all the Devarshis, I am Narad."

The term Maharshi occurring in the sixth section of the *Ramayana*, the learned translators subjoin the following note: "There are four kinds of sages, or Rishis: the Rajarshi or royal sage; the Maharshi, or great sage; the Brahmarshi, or sacred sage; and the Devarshi, or divine sage; of these the first is esteemed the lowest, and the last the highest."

According to the *Ramayana*, Sura means any fermented liquor; and Asura, rejecting spirituous liquors. Describing the well known allegory of churning the ocean, that will be particularly noticed hereafter, "the daughter of Varuna, Varuni," is produced; and said, in a note, to be spirituous liquors "seeking for acceptance. The sons of Diti did not receive the daughter of Varuna; upon which the sons of Aditi accepted the inestimable damsel. On this occasion, therefore, are the descendants of Diti called Asuras, while descendants of Aditi are termed Suras." By the reception of Varuni the glad Suras were filled with pleasure."

When, in the course of this churning process, the Amrita, the water of immortality, was produced, the Suras and Asuras contended for its possession; and a tremendous combat ensued between them. "When all were exhausted, Vishnu, the mighty, assuming by illusion the form of a captivating damsel, speedily stole the Amrita," and afterwards crushed the Asuras, or sons of Diti. "In this most dreadful conflict between the Daityas and the celestials, the former being subdued, Purandara received the kingdom." Purandara is a name of Indra.

Many other benevolent and malevolent races of spiritual beings are enumerated in the *Ramayana* and other Hindu authorities. The Siddhas, of whom there were eight only; the Gandharvas, Kinnaras, Dundhubis, who are numerous, and appear to be choristers, dancers, flower-showerers, and other pleasant companions; and the Rakshas, Yakshas, are generally in malignant combinations: though not, however, always; these good and evil genii appear to change characters, For instance, sometimes Yakshas are benevolent, or at least classed with good beings, sometimes malignant. Danavas are also good and at other times, "evil genii, at enmity with the gods."

Apsaras

Another race of angelic creatures, although most ungallantly neglected in mythological fable, we must not pass by unnoticed. These are the interesting, the beautiful, Apsaras: they are proverbially elegant and graceful; but, alas! not so for virtue or morals.

These fair maids were produced when the ocean was churned in the time of the

Kurmavatara; in number no less than six hundred millions! of resplendent and celestial form; "adorned with glorious ornaments, and endowed with beauty, youth, sweetness, and every grace." Their female attendants were innumerable; but "not having undergone the legal purification, none of the gods, or Danavas, received these damsels in marriage; hence they all remained without a lord."

Thus we find the Hindu invisible world well peopled but there are several other tribes of mythological beings introduced into the complicated machinery of Hindu poetics. There is a race, no bigger than a man's thumb, called Balakhilya, of whom sixty thousand were produced from the hairs of Brahma's body; and another race of Lilliputian sages, produced from his nails.

All of these beings are by name, birth, parentage, and education; life, death, and burial, etc., especially chronicled in the Puranas, and other sacred and prophane books; and one's brain is almost bewildered in endeavouring to trace their genealogy, character, connections, and a long train of etceteras, combined with their allegorical origin, progress, and termination.

Daksha

The name of Daksha occurs several times in the course of my work; and, as a good deal of mythological legend is attached to it, I shall collect in this place what I have extracted from the *Asiatic Researches* relative to that character:

"Iswara attempted to kill his brother Brahma who, being immortal, was only maimed; but Iswara finding him afterwards in a mortal shape, in the character of Daksha, killed him as he was performing a sacrifice."

The following is a continuation of the legend from Hindu sacred books:

There had subsisted for a long time some animosity between Brahma and Mahadeva in their mortal shapes; and the latter, on account of his bad conduct, which is fully described in the Puranas, had, it appears, given much uneasiness to Swayambhuva and Satarupa: for he was libidinous, going about with a large club in his hand. Mahadeva was the eldest, and was indignant at seeing his claim as such disregarded in favour of Brahma, which the latter supported by such lies as provoked Mahadeva to such a point, that he cut off one of his heads in his divine form. In his human shape, we find Daksha boasting that he ruled over mankind.

One day, in the assembly of the gods, Daksha coming in, they all respectfully arose except Mahadeva, who kept his seat, and looked gloomy, which Daksha resented; and reviled and cursed Mahadeva in his human shape, wishing he might ever remain a vagabond on the face of the earth; and ordered that he should be avoided, and deprived of his share of the sacrifices and offerings. Mahadeva, irritated, in his turn, cursed Daksha; and a dreadful conflict took place between them: the three worlds trembled, and the gods were alarmed. Brahma, Vishnu, and the whole assembly interfered, and separated the combatants; and, at length, even effected a reconciliation. In consequence of which, Daksha gave one of his daughters, named Sati, in marriage to Mahadeva: Sati was an incarnation of Devi; for Sridevi, the wife of Daksha, and daughter of Adima and Iva, entreated the goddess to give her one daughter exactly like herself.

Her request was granted; and Devi was incarnated in her womb, and, was born as Sati. Sridevi had besides a hundred daughters, but no son, which she and Daksha deeply lamented; and agreed to make a solemn sacrifice to obtain one. On this occasion Daksha convened gods and men, omitting, however, Mahadeva, who took but little notice of the neglect; for he is represented in all his Avataras as indifferent to praise or abuse. But his wife Sati insisted on going, and could not be dissuaded; and was treated so contemptuously by her father, Daksha, that she flung herself into the fire, and thereby spoiled the sacrifice. Mahadeva, hearing this, blamed her for her rash conduct, thus spoiling a religious sacrifice, and cursed her; and consequently was doomed for a transmigration of a thousand years, into an inferior being. Thus she become a Pika (a sort of bird of the Cuckoo tribe); and Mahadeva, to please her, assumed the form of a Pikas, under the title of Pikeswara, or Pikesa-Mahadeva.

Mahadeva afterwards went up to Brahma, in the character of Daksha, and after much abuse began to beat him; the confusion became general in the assembly, who all took the part of Daksha; but Siva, striking the ground with the locks of his Jata, produced two heroes, and an army of demons came to his assistance; the battle raged, and in the general conflict Mahadeva cut off Daksha's head: several of the gods were wounded, particularly the Sun and Moon; heaven, hell, and the earth trembled.

The gods at last humbled themselves before Mahadeva, who was appeased, and order was restored. At their request he promised to restore Daksha to life; but the head could not be found; during the fray it fell into the fire and was burnt. A he goat was then brought, and his head was struck off and placed on the lifeless body of Daksha, who instantly revived; but he remained weak and powerless, till he was again born.

Mahadeva, taking up the body of his beloved Sati, carried it seven times round the world, bewailing his misfortune.

The gods whom Sati contained in her womb burst out; her limbs were scattered all over the world; and the places where they fell are become sacred. Her breasts fell near Jalandhar in the Panjab; the Yoni into Assam; and the Guhya into Nepal; where they are most devoutly worshipped to this day; the latter is a small cleft in a rock, with an intermitting spring; it is called Guhyasthan.

Mr. Paterson thinks the fable refers to an unsuccessful attempt to abolish the worship of the male and female symbols; and invented by the Saivas to show the imbecility of their opponents, and to exalt their own doctrines; the gods themselves being introduced as actors instead of their votaries.

And Daksha, on condition of embracing the doctrine of Siva, was restored to life, degraded with the head of a goat instead of his own.

Prithu and Prithivi, and Viswakarma

Prithivi is the goddess of the Earth; Viswakarma, the artificer of the universe, that is, the lord of creation assuming that character, moulded the earth, and it became Prithivi—conspicuous; and therefore is that name, Prithivi, assigned to the earth. Prithu is her husband: he was an incarnation of Vishnu.

Vena, being an impious and tyrannical prince, was cursed by the Brahmins and in consequence died without issue. To remedy this his left arm was opened, and churned with a stick till it produced a son; who, proving as wicked as his father, was set aside; and the right arm was in like manner churned, which also produced a boy, who proved to be a form of Vishnu under the name of Prithu.

Gods and men came to make obeisance to him and to celebrate his appearance on earth. He married a form of the goddess Lakshmi, who was thence named Prithivi or Prithwi, and was in fact the earth; and at this time refused so obstinately to give her wonted supplies to mankind, that Prithu was forced to beat and wound her; when she (the earth), assuming the form of a cow, ascended to Meru to complain to the gods; who rejected her complaint. Prithu and his descendants were allowed to beat and wound her in cases of noncompliance; and the earth reluctantly submitted; and since that time mankind are continually wounding her with ploughs and other implements of husbandry.

Prithu was fond of agriculture, became a husbandman, cut down forests, levelled the earth, etc.; which is to be understood by his quarrel with the earth.

Prithivi is one of the deities whom daily sacrifices are offered by Brahmins, to the manes of deceased ancestors. They are numerated in the *Book of Manu.*

"To Kuhu, goddess of the day, when the new moon is discernible; to Anumati, goddess of the day, after the opposition; to Prajapati, or the lord of creatures; to Dyava and Prithivi, goddesses of sky and earth; and, lastly, to the fire of the good sacrifice."

Pritihivi, as a personification of the earth, also represents Patience: the Hindus refer to the earth, or Prithivi, proverbially, as an example of patience, or forbearance; permitting her bowels to be ripped open, her surface lacerated, and suffering every indignity without resentment or murmuring. She is quoted also as an example of correctness; as returning good for evil. Prithivipati, i.e., Lord of the Earth, is a title conferred on terrestrial, or real, as well as mythological, sovereigns.

Sir W. Jones thinks Viswakarma to be the Vulcan of the Greeks and being, like Vulcan, the forger of arms for the gods and inventor of the Agnyastra, or fire-shaft, in the war between them, and the Daityas, or Titans.

He is deemed the architect of the universe, and chief engineer of the gods. He revealed the fourth Upaveda in various treatises on sixty-four mechanical arts; for the improvement of such as exercise them; and he is the inspector of all manual labours and mechanical arts.

Viswakarma seems to have some reference to the Varahavatara. The following passage, from the Black Yajurveda says:

"Waters alone there were; this world originally was water. In it the lord of creation moved, having become air, he saw this earth and upheld it, assuming the form of a boar, Varaha, and then moulded that earth, becoming Viswakarma, the artificer of the universe. It became celebrated and conspicuous (Prithivi) and therefore is that name Prithivi assigned to the earth."

By most accounts he was employed by Krishna to build for him the city of Dwarka, in Gujarat, when forced to quit his beloved Mathura. He had a daughter, named Barhismati, but I know nothing of her. The name or title Viswakarma means, I believe, the all-performing—factotum.

• • •

7

Yama, Sani, Vrihaspati

Yama

Yama is a very important deity: his name occurs frequently in the sacrificial ceremonies of the Hindus; oblations and invocations to him, forming a portion of several of these ceremonies. He is regent of the south, or low world, in which the Hindus place the infernal regions; thus corresponding, as the judge of departed souls with the Grecian Pluto or **Minos. Minos has been supposed as the same with Manu; with whom, especially with the seventh, Satyavrata,** Yama also agrees in character, as welt as in name; both being called Vaivaswata, or offspring of the Sun, and Sraddhadeva, or lord of the Sraddha. Sraddha is the ceremonial oblation in honour of deceased ancestors; which obsequies to the manes are attended with feasting, and various observances of curious and singular description. Yama has many names: Dharmaraja, or king of justice; Pitripati, or lord of the pitris, or patriarchs; Mrityu, or Death, or Kala. Susanyama, and Vaivaswata Yama are derivatives: the first from a word implying comeliness, or beauty; the other from his solar origin. Audumbara is a name derived from a species of wood, by the attrition of which fire is produced, wherewith to light the pile on which funereal obsequies are performed to Yama.

His abode is in the infernal city of Yamapur, whither the Hindus believe that a departed soul immediately repairs; and receiving a just sentence from Yama, ascends on Swarga, the first heaven, or descends to Naraka, the snaky hell; or assumes on earth the form of some animal, vegetable, or even to a mineral prison.

Yama, the regent of hell, has two dogs, according to the Puranas: one of them named Cerbura, or varied; the other, Syama, or black: the first is also called Trisiras, or with three heads; **Cerbura is indubitably the Cerberus of the Greeks.**

Dharmaraja, or the king of justice, has two countenances: one called his divine countenance, mild, and full of benevolence; and those only see it who abound in virtue. His other countenance, or form, is called Yama; this the wicked alone can see: it has large teeth and a monstrous look. Yama is lord of Patala, or the infernal regions: there he orders some to be beaten, some to be cut to pieces, some to be devoured by monsters, etc. His servant is named Kashmala, who drags the wicked, with ropes round their necks over rugged paths, and throws them headlong into hell.

The fourteenth day of the dark half of the month Aswina is called Yamatarpanam and is sacred to Yama: bathing and libations are auspicious on that day; and on the following torches and flaming brands are kindled, and consecrated to burn the bodies of kinsmen who may be dead in battle, or in a foreign country, and to light them through the shades of death to the mansions of Yama.

The second day of the following month, Kartika, is also sacred to Yama, conjointly with his youngest sister, the river goddess Yamuna, she having entertained her brother on that day: in imitation of which, sisters give entertainments to, and receive presents from, their brothers.

But, in the tenth book of the Rig Veda, Yamuna is called the twin sister of Yama; and a dialogue is given, in which he endeavours to seduce her, but his base offers are rejected by her with virtuous expostulation.

Krishna, in the *Gita*, says to Arjun, "Among all those who rule, I am Yama," implying superiority on the part of Yama.

That very interesting and affecting ceremony, called Sraddha, is an oblation of daily recurrence with individuals who rigidly adhere to the ritual. It is offered in honour of deceased ancestors—but not merely in honour of them but for their comfort. Over these ceremonials presides Yama.

The priests meditate the Gayatri, and thrice repeat—"Salutation to the gods, to the manes of ancestors, and to mighty saints; to Swaha (goddess of fire) and Swadha (the food of the manes). Salutation to them for ever and ever."

In the third chapter of the Book of Manu the rules for the performance of the Sraddha are detailed with prolixity:

"Let the housekeeper who knows his duty perform each day a Sraddha with boiled rice and the like, or with water, or with milk, roots, and fruit; for thus he obtains favour from departed progenitors.

"Sages have distinguished the monthly Sraddha by the title of Anwaharya or after-eaten; that is, eaten after the pinda or ball of rice: and it must be performed with extreme care, and with flesh meat in the best condition."

"At the Sraddha of the gods, he may entertain two Brahmins; at that of his father, paternal grandfather, and a paternal great-grandfather, three; or only one at that of the gods, and one at that of his paternal ancestors. Though he abound in wealth, let him not be solicitous to entertain a large company.

"As many mouthfuls of an unlearned man shall swallow at an oblation to the gods and to ancestors, so many red-hot iron balls must the giver of the Sraddha swallow in the next world.

Of the gift at a Sraddha, to as many Brahmins as a sacrificer for a Sudra might be able to touch on the body, the fruit is lost to the giver if he invite such a wretch.

"Should the eater of a Sraddha enter on the same day the bed of a seducing woman, his ancestors would sleep for that month on her excrement.

"Having, by the word Swaditam, asked the Brahmins if they have eaten well, let him give them, being satisfied, water or an ablution.

"Then let the Brahmins address him, saying Swadha; for in all ceremonies relating to deceased ancestors, the word Swadha is the highest benison."

Swadha is a goddess, whose adventures are very poetically narrated in the *Brahma-vaivarta Purana,* originally a nymph of Goloka, the paradise of Vishnu. She is the goddess of funeral obsequies; conveying to the manes the offerings of men, and rewarding the latter for their piety to ancestors.

A dying man, when no hopes of his surviving remain, should be laid on a bed of Kusa grass in the open air, his head sprinkled with water drawn from the Ganges, and smeared with clay brought from the same river. A Salagrama stone should be placed near him, holy strains from the Veda should be chanted aloud, and leaves of holy basil scattered over his head.

When he expires, the corpse must be washed, perfumed, and decked with wreaths of flowers, and carried by the nearest relations to some spot in the forest, or near water: the funeral-pile is lighted from the consecrated fire maintained by the deceased; the nearest relation applies the flaming brand to the pile, and the attendant priests recite the appropriate invocations.—"Fire! thou wast lighted by him; may he, therefore, be reproduced from thee, that he may attain the regions of celestial bliss. May this offrering be auspicious." All who followed the corpse walk round the pile, but may not view the fire: they then proceed to the river, and after bathing present oblations of water from the joined palms of their hands to the manes of the deceased, saying, "May this oblation reach thee." Elegiac verses, are then recited.

"Foolish is he who seek for permanence in the human state; in solid, like the stem of the plantain tree; transient, like the foam of the sea.

"When a body, formed of five elements, to receive the reward of deeds done in its own former person, reverts to its five original principles, what room is there for regret?

"The earth is perishable; the ocean, the gods themselves, pass away.—How should not that bubble, mortal man; meet destruction?

"All that is low must finally perish; all that is elevated must ultimately fall; all compounded bodies must end in dissolution; and life be concluded with death."

Sani

Sani is described in some passages of the Puranas as clad in a black mantle. with a dark turban loosely wrapped round his head; his aspect hideous, and his brows knit with anger; a trident in one of his four hands, a cemeter in a second, and in the other two, a bow and shafts, mounted on an elephant.

Sani

The elephant has been thought an appropriate vehicle for the sluggish "slow-moving son of Surya," as referring to the immense scope of Saturn's orbit, and the apparent slowness of his motion. And Sani being, among the astrologers of India, as well as with their sapient brethren of Europe, a planet of malignant aspects, the ill-omened raven may also be deemed a fit vahan for such a dreaded being. Both in England and in India, the raven is so rare a bird. It breeds every year, like the crow, and is much longer lived; and while the latter bird abounds everywhere to a degree bordering on nuisance, a pair of ravens, for they are seldom seen singly or in trios, are not found duplicated in any place. Perhaps one or two pairs of ravens will not be found on an average extent of five hundred or a thousand acres. Why? That raven destroys its young; we shall at once see the propriety of symbolising it with Saturn. or Kronos, or Time, devouring or destroying his own offspring.

Vrihaspati

Of Vrihaspati, the regent of the planet Jupiter, we shall say but little, although he is in fact an important person, especially in astronomical calculations. In mere mythology, I have only to notice him as the preceptor to the gods, their occasional messenger from one to another. Vrihaspati is supposed to have been also a legislator and a philosopher and thus to have given his name and character to the planet, in which Siva himself is said also to shine.

• • •

8

Linga and Yoni

Linga

The mystery in which the real history of these emblems of nature is veiled, renders it extremely difficult to give a clear account of the origin or tendency of the rites by which we see their votaries honour them. That they had their origin in nature and innocence we may admit, without admitting likewise of the propriety of their continuance to a period when nature and innocence are no longer seen unsophisticated; knowing, howevcr, so little of the genuine history of these rites and symbols, it is but a reasonable extension of charity to suppose that their origin was philosophical, though mysterious, and that their observance, although offensive, is not criminal.

It is some comparative and negative praise to the Hindus, that the emblems, under which they exhibit the elements and operations of nature, are not externally indecorous. **Unlike the abominable realities of Egypt and Greece, we see the phallic emblem in the**

llindu Pantheon without offence; and know not, until the information be extorted, that we are contemplating a symbol whose prototype is indelicate. Their views may be examined, over and over, and the uninformed obsener will not be aware that he has viewed the typical representation of the generative organs or powers of humanity. The external decency of the symbols, and the difficulty with which their recondite allusions are discovered, both offer evidence favourable to the moral delicacy of the Hindu character.

The subject of the Linga and Yoni, being in itself very curious, and the diffculty of obtaining authentic information thereon evident, I shall take the liberty of borrowing at some length from the learned and ingenious dissertation, by Mr. Wilford, *On Egypt and the Nile, From the Sacred Books of the Hindus,* an interesting portion, illustrating the dark subjects in question; or if not fully illustrating them, showing, at any rate, their mysteriousness,and wildness of the allegories referring to them, which even his power of research seems scarcely competent to reach.

Linga, the symbol of the regenerator, Siva be recollected, is the *membrum virile*: the phallic emblem of the Greeks. The symbol of the female power, Siva's Sakti, or energy, Paravati, who on this mystical occasion is more commonly called Devi, is the Yoni; otherwise Bhaga, *pudendum muliebre.*

The Worship of Linga and Yoni

Speaking of Bhavani as distinguished by a variety of names implyhlg nature, and, among others, using that of Shakti, Paolino, in his *Voyage*, gives an account of the Magna Mater of the Hindus; he says, she changes and transforms herself into a thousand shapes, and appears sometimes as a man and sometimes as a woman. I have introduced this author here to notice his observation, that on her forehead, as well as on their own, her votaries "paint the Yoni, or Medhra; which is represented by two side strokes, and a red one in the middle."

He uses the word Medhra again: describing the marks on the forehead, etc., that Hindus distinguish their sect by; he says, that the mark of Devi's sectaries is made of three strokes; the lateral, white or yellow, the middle always red. This mark represents the Medhra, that is, the womb of Bhavani, from which everything existing was produced: it is much used by the Shivaites and Vishnuvites.

This word Medhra is new to me, and is, I suppose, a term used in Malabar, similar to Yoni.

A general war is often mentioned in the Puranas, and was celebrated by the poets of the West as the basis of the Grecian mythology: the war in question arose between both Nonnus and the Hindu mythologists; it began in India, whence it was spread over the whole globe; and all mankind appears to have borne a part in it.

These religious and physiological contests were disguised in Egypt and India under a veil of the wildest allegories and emblems. On the banks of the Nile, Osiris was torn into pieces; and on those of the Ganges, the limbs of Isi, or Sati, were scattered over the world, giving names to the places where they fell, and where they are superstitiously worshipped. There is a legend in the Sarvarasa, of which the figurative meaning is more obvious. When Sati, after the close of her existence as the daughter of Daksha, sprang again to life in the character of Parvati or mountain-born, she was reunited in marriage to Mahadeva.

This divine pair had once a dispute on the comparative influence of sexes in producing animated beings; and each resolved, by mutual agreement, to create apart a new race of men. The race produced by Mahadeva was very numerous. and devoted themselves exclusively to the worshlp of the male deity; but their intellects were dull, their bodies feeble. tbeir limbs distorted. and their complexions of different hues. Parvati had at the same time created a multitude of human beings, who adored the female power only and were all well shaped, with sweet aspects and fine complexions.

A furious contest eusued between the two races, and the Lingajas were defeated in battle by the Yonijas. But Mahadeva, enraged against the Yonijas would have destroyed them with the fire of his eye, if Parvati had not interposed and appeased him;

but he would spare them only on condition that they should instantly quit the country, to return no more. And from the Yoni, which they adored as the sole cause of their existence, they were named Yavanas.

It is evident that the strange tale from the *Sarvarasa* was invented to establish the opinion of the Yonyankitas, or votaries of Devi, that the good shape, strength and courage of animals depend on the superlor influence of the female parent, whose powers are only excited, or put into action, by the male aura. But the Lingankitas maintain an opposite doctrine; and proofs in support of their opinion might be brought, from many examples in the animal and vegetable worlds. There is also a sect of Hindus, by far the most numerous of any. who, attempting to reconcile the two systems, tell us, in their allegorical style, that Parvati and Mahadeva found their concurrence essential to the perfection of their offspring; and that Vishnu at the request of the goddess, effected a reconciliation between them; hence the navel of Vishnu is worshipped as one and the same with the sacred Yoni.

Another of their emblems is called Argha, which means a cup, or dish, or any other vessel in which fruit and flowers are offered to the deities, and which ought always to be shaped like a boat; though we now see Arghas of many different forms—oval, circular, or square; and hence it is that Iswara has the title of Arghanatha, or Lord of the Boat-shaped Vessel.

A rim round the Argha represents the mysterious Yoni, and the navel of Vishnu is commonly denoted by a convexity in the centre, while the contents of the vessel are symbols of the Linga.

I shall insert, some of the legends, on the subject of the Linga, Yoni, Argha, etc.

One day, as Mahadeva was rambling over the earth, naked, he chanced to pass near the spot where several Munis were performing their devotions. Mahadeva laughed at them, and insulted them in very provoking and indecent terms, enforcing his abuse by significant signs and gestures. The offended Munis cursed him; and the Linga, or Phallus, fell to the ground. Mahadeva, in this state of mutilation, travelled over the world, bewailing his misfortune; his consort too gave herself up to grief, and followed him in a state of distraction, repeating mournful songs. This, Mr. Wilford says, is what the Greek mythologists call the wanderings of Dematur, and the lamentations of Bacchus.

The world being thus deprived of its vivifying principle, generation and vegetation were at a stand; gods and men were alarmed; and having discovered the cause of it, searched for, and found, the sacred Linga, grown to an immense size, and endowed with life and motion.

Having worshipped the sacred pledge, they cut it into thirty-one pieces; which, polypus-like each became a perfect Linga. The Devatas left one and twenty of them on earth, carried nine to heaven, and one to the inferior regions, for the benefit of the inhabitants of the three worlds, to satisfy Devi, and restore all things to their former situation. Mahadeva was born again, in the character of Baleswara or Iswara the infant; but suddenly became a man, under the title of Lileswara, or Iswara who gives delight; and after various adventures, met his consort then in the character of Samirama, (the Semiramis of the Greeks); who, by the sweetness of her voice in chanting her own metamorphosis and that of Lileswara, attracted the notice of her former and future spouse in his present character—till now, entirely indifferent to the female sex. The goddess soon became Lileswari, and was happily reunited to her Lord.

In the dreadful war, above mentioned, between the Lingankitas and Yonijas, the former stood their ground pretty well at first, but were in the end defeated. and shamefully routed in the battle, through the potency of the sacred Yoni. Mahadeva, enraged, was about to destroy them by tbe fire of his eye; but Parvati interposed, and, to appease him, made use of the same artifice that Baubo did to put Ceres into good humour; and showed him the prototype of the Lotus; Mahadeva smiled, and relented, on condition that the Yonijas should instantly leave the country. **Whether this legend alludes to a real war between the worshippers of the Linga and**

Yoni, or be a mere physiological allegory, could not be determined.

During the general deluge, Brahma, or the creative power, was asleep at the bottom of the abyss; the generative powers of nature, both male and female, reduced to their simplest elements, the Linga and the Yoni assumed the shape of the hull of a ship, since typified by the Argha, whilst the Linga became the mast. In this manner they were wafted over the deep under the care and protection of Vishnu.

At the very extremity of a promontory on the island of Bombay, called Malabar Point, is a cleft rock, a fancied resemblance of the Yoni, to which numerous pilgrims and persons resort for the purpose of regeneration by the efficacy of a passage through this sacred type. This Yoni, or hole, is of considerable elevation, situated among rocks, of no easy access, and, in the stormy season, incessantly buffetted by the surf of the ocean. Near it are the ruins of a temple, that present appearances warrant us to conclude, was formerly of rather an elegant description. It is said, with probability, to have been blown up by gun powder, by the pious zeal of the idol-hating Portuguese, while Bombay was under their flag.

Fragments of well-hewn stone are now seen scattered over and around its site, having a variety of images sculptured on their surface. I have particularly examined its remains; and, with the help of my servants, succeeded in removing the stones and rubbish from the surface of the ground, and discovering what was buried beneath. The temple appears to have been sacred to the Hindu Trinity in Unity; for I found a stone, a good deal mutilated, some feet uuder the ground and ruins, well carved into the triform head so stupendously sculptured in the cave at Dharapuri, or Elephanta. The stone thus found seems a fair model of its gigantic neighbour. The fragment is more than two feet high, nearly as broad, and about eighteen inches thick, and is of course very heavy. I brought this stone to England, and it is now deposited in the Company's museum at the India House. The front face is Brahma; on his right, Siva; to his left, Vishnu.

The cleft or Yoni at Malabar Point is a type much resorted to. When Raghoba, the father of the present Baji Rao, while exiled from Poona, was living in Bombay, he fixed his residence on Malabar hill, where he built a lofty habitable tower, since removed. He was in the habit occasionally of passing through the cleft and, being a Brahmin of comsiderable piety, was doubtless much benefited by such regeneration. It is related of Sivaji, that he has been known to venture secretly on the island of Bombay, to avail himself of the benefit of this efficacious transit. Women also, as well as men, go through this operation; and I have witnessed some distressing scenes in the unsuccessful effort of individuals, loaded either with sin or flesh, or both.

It is necessary to descend some steps on rugged rocks, and then; by first protruding the hands, you ascend head first up the hole. After the feet be lifted from their last support, the ascent is very difficult, and sometimes impracticable; in which case the person remains with his head and hands exposed to the laughing or commiserating spectators above; and it is necessary that some one should go below to aid the disappointed aspirant in his or her descent. I have several times attempted this regeneration, but could never effect it; although I have often seen my superiors in bulk and, I conclude, in skill, as well as faith and good works, perform it with apparent ease.

Another instance of piety of the aforesaid I have heard that a cow of gold was made, but it may have been only an image of smaller dimensions; and that Raghoba himself also was passed through the typical Yoni.

While in the exile before noticed, he sent two Brahmins on an embassy to England; they went by sea to Suez, and returned by Persia. On their return, they were treated as outcasts; for, although men of unexceptionable character, it was deemed impossible for them to travel through countries inhabited by Mlechhas, or impure tribes, and live according to the rules laid down in their sacred books.

After various consultations among learned Brahmins, convened from all parts, it was decreed by the holy assembly, that, in consideration of the good character of the travellers, and the motive of their journey, which was the good of their country, they might be regenerated, and have their sacerdotal ordination renewed. For the purpose of regeneration, it is directed to make an image of pure gold of the female power of nature, in the shape either of a woman or a cow; in this statue the person to be regenerated is enclosed, and is dragged out through the usual channel. As a statue of pure gold, and of proper dimensions, would have been too expensive, it was deemed sufficient to make an image of the sacred Yoni. Raghoba accordingly had one made of pure gold; and his ambassadors having been regenerated by passing through it, with proper ceremonies, including presents to the Brahmins, were readmitted into the communion of the faithful.

• • •

9

Sakti

It has been noticed, that the principal attributes of the Deity, Brahma, Vishnu, and Siva, have consorts assigned them; which consorts are personifications respectively of the active energies of their lords, and are called Sakti. Saraswati is the Sakti of Brahma, Lakshmi of Vishnu, and Parvati of Siva; hence those, of whatever sect, who worship exclusively the female power—Paravati, i.e., Devi—however, more especially, are called the Saktas. Not only are the three great powers so accommodated, the inferior deities in their own persons and the Avataras of the superior, are likewise mated in fable, and have their wills executed by active helpmates; each of whom, except in sex, exactly resembles the deity whose partner she is.

Eight of these Saktis are more particularly recorded:

Maheswari	the Sakti of Mahesa, or Siva.
Brahmi, or Brahmani	the Sakti of Brahma.
Narayani	the Sakti of Narayana.
Aindri	the Sakti of Indra.

Kaumari	the Sakti of Kartikeya.
Varahi	the Sakti of Vishnu in the Vaharavatara.
Narasinghani	the Sakti of Vishnu in the Narasingh Avatara.
Aparajita	a form of Bhavani; the female principle.

This list is taken from Mr. Paterson's *Essay on the Origin of the Hindu Religion.* The last, Mr. Paterson remarks, may be the Aphrodite of the Greeks; and Maheswari, or a female Siva, riding on a white bull, may have given rise to the story of Europa's rape; while Brahmi, or the female Brahma, with the swan, may, in like manner, have occasioned the fable of Jupiter and Leda. These explanations were, perhaps, invented by the Greeks, to account for symbols, of the meaning of which they were ignorant.

On the foregoing passage Mr. Colebrooke gives a note, containing the following information:

The eight Saktis, or energies of as many deities, are also called Matris, or mothers. They are called Brahmi, etc., because they sprung from the bodies of Brahma and the other gods respectively.

In some places they are thus enumerated: Brahmi, Maheswari, Aindri, Varahi, Vaishnavi, Kaumari, Chamunda, and Charchika. Some reduce the number to seven, omitting the two latter, and adding Kuveri.

Prayers are addressed to the Matris on various occasions, especially in the Kavachas, or defensive incantations. I shall cite two by way of example, and subjoin extracts, from

Kali, the Goddes of Death

the *Markandeya Purana*, descriptive of these goddesses:

"May Brahmani, conferring the benefit of all benedictions, protect me on the east; and Narayani on the south-east, for the sake of realising every wish; Maheswari too on the south, rendering everything auspicious; Chamunda on the south-west, discomfiting all enemies; and, on the west Kaumari, armed with her lance, and slayer of foes: on the north-west Aparajita, the beauteous giver of victory; on the north Varahi, granter of boons; and, on the north-east, Narasinghi, the banisher of terror. May these mothers, being eight deities and active powers, defend me."

Another incantation simply enumerates the same eight goddesses, and proceeds thus:

"May these, and all Matris, guard me with their respective weapons on all quarters, and on every point."

In the *Devi Mahatmya* the assembling of the Matris to combat the demons is thus described:

"The energy of each god, exactly like him, with the same form, tbe same decoration, and the same vehicle, came to fight against the demons. The Sakti of Brahma, girt with a white gourd, arrived on a car yoked with swans: her title is Brahmani. Maheswari came riding on a bull, and bearing a trident, with a vast serpent for a ring, and a crescent for a gem. Kaumari, bearing a lance in her hand, and riding on a peacock, being Ambika, in the form of Kartikeya, came to make war on the children of Diti. The Sakti named Vaishnavi also arrived,

Goddess Durga

sitting on an eagle, and bearing a conch, a discus, a club,and a bow, and a sword in her several hands. The energy of Hari, who assumed the unrivaled form of the holy boar, likewise came there, assuming the body of Varahi. Narasinghi too arrived there, embodied in a form precisely similar to that of Nrisinhi, with an erect mane reaching to the host of stars. Aindri came, bearing the thunderbolt in her hand, and riding on the king of elephants, and in every respect like Indra, with a hundred eyes. Lastly came the dreadful energy named Chandika, who sprung from the body of Devi, horrible, howling like a hundred shakals; she, surnamed Aparajita, the unconquered goddess, thus addressed Isani, whose head is encircled with his dusky braided locks."

The story, which is too long for insertion in this place, closes with these words: "Thus did the wrathful host of Matris slay the demons."

In the *Uttara Kalpa*, of the same Purana, the Matris are thus described: "Chamunda standing on a corpse; Varahi sitting on a buffalo; Aindri mounted on an elephant; Vaishnavi borne by an eagle; Maheswari riding on a bull; Kaumari conveyed by a peacock; Brahmi carried by a swan; and Aparajita revered by the universe; are all Matris endowed with every faculty."

It may be proper to notice, that Chamunda, Charchika, and Chandika, are all forms of Parvati. According to one legend, Chamunda sprung from the frown of Parvati to slay the demons Chanda and Munda; according to another, the mild portion of Parvati issued from her side, leaving the wrathful portion, which constitutes Kali, or the black goddess.

Kuveri is the energy of Kuvera, the deformed god of riches. Narayani, mentioned by Mr. Paterson, and also in the prayers or incantations above cited, is the same with Vaishnavi.

1. Brahma	Brahmi or Saraswati,	the swan, or goose.
2. Vishnu	Vaishnavi or Lakshmi,	(generally) Garuda.
In his character or Avatara of	Lakshmi, under her several names of	
Varaha	Varahi,	a buffalo, or a bear
Narasingha	Nrisinhi	
Narayana	Narayani	
3. Rudra Maheswara	Rudri, Maheswari,	a bull; the Sakti sometimes on a tiger
	And several other names of Siva and Bhavani	
4. Indra	Indrani,	the elephant Iravata
5. Vaishnavi, or Lakshmi,	Kumari	a peacock
6. Kuvera	Kuveri	

In the thirteenth section of the *Ramayana* the company assembled at an Aswamedha, or sacrifice of a horse, is enumerated, and the following passage occurs: "Thither were previously collected the gods, the sages, etc., for the sake of receiving their respective shares. Brahma too, the sovereign of the gods, with Sthanu and Narayana, chief of beings, and the four supporters of the universe, and the divine mothers of all the celestials, met together there."—A note on this passage informs us, that the "four supporters of the universe" are Indra, regent of the east; Yama, of the south; Varuna, of the west; and Kuvera, of the north." "The divine mothers of the celestials" are stated to "be seven: Brahmi, Maheswari, Rudri, Komari, Vaishnavi, Varahi and Indrani." The supporters of the universe are considered in future pages; and I will here enumerate, or recapitulate, the names of the Saktis, or Matris, of the different deities that occur to me as being so mated; addiing, also, the vahan or vehicle by which such power, male or female, is conveyed.

I, therefore, make out but six separate Saktis, or Matris; and as one of them, Kumari, is understood to be the same with Ambika, a name or form of Devi, (or Bhavani, or Parvati, the reputed mother of Kartikeya, or Kumara,) they may be reduced to five; and, indeed, as all the gods are resolvable into three, and ultimately into one, so, similarly, are their Saktis or consorts.

I have hitherto made, and found, no distinction between Sakti and Matri; but I am of opinion that there is some difference, although I do not know what it is. Several deities have Saktis as well as those above enumerated, whose names there are no authorities for adding to the list as Matris: Sita, for instance, is called the Sakti of Rama; Radha of Krishna; Chandri of Chandra; Swaha of Agni; Prithivi of Prithu; Niriti of Nirut; Varuni of Varuna; and although their names do not occur in any of the foregoing lists, they are considered, generally, as the Saktis, or the subordinate powers, or energies, of their respective lords.

• • •

Devi is the greatest: No gender bias

10

Kama Deva, God of Love

Notwithstanding the popularity of this deity In India where, both in poetry and conversation, Kama is, as in most other refined countries, in person, or by allusion to his attributes and effects, so often introduced, I do not find one representation of Kama among my images or pictures; nor do I recollect ever having seen an original in India.

Sir William Jones says:

"The Hindu god, to whom the hymn is addressed, appears evidently the same with the Grecian Eros and the Roman Cupid: but the Indian description of his person and arms, his family, attendants, and attributes, has new and peculiar beauties.

"According to the mythology of Hindustan, he was the son of Maya, or the general attracting power, married to Rati, or Affection; and his bosom friend is Basant, or Spring. He is represented as a beautiful youth, sometimes conversing with his mother and consort in the midst of his gardens and temples; sometimes riding by moonlight on a parrot or lory, and attended by dancing girls or nymphs, the foremost of whom bears his colours, which are a fish on a red ground. His bow of sugarcane, or flowers, with a string formed of bees, and his five arrows, each pointed with an Indian blossom of a healing quality, are equally new and beautiful. He has at least twenty-three names; that of Kama, signifies desire. The story alludes to the bold attempt of this deity to wound the great god Mahadeva, for which he was punished by a flame consuming his corporeal nature, and reducing him to a mental essence; and hence his chief dominion is over the minds of mortals, or such deities as he is permitted to subdue."

Poets perpetually recur to this mishap of Kama. Here follows some farther notice of that celebrated event.

Mahadeva and Parvati, playing with dice at the game of Chaturanga (chess) disputed, and parted in wrath; and severally performing rigid acts of devotion to the Supreme Being, kindled thereby such vehement fires as threatened a general conflagration. The Devas, in great alarm, hastened to Brahma; who led them to Mahadeva, and supplicated him to recall his consort; but the wrathful god answered, that she must return to him of her own free choice. They accordingly deputed Ganga, the river goddess, who prevailed on Parvati to return to her husband, on the condition that his love for her should be restored.

The celestial mediators then employed Kamadeva, who wounded Siva with one of his flowery arrows; but the angry deity reduced the god of love to ashes. Parvati, soon after, presented herself before Siva in the semblance of a Kirati, daughter of a mountaineer; and seeing him enamoured of her, assumed her own shape, and effected a reunion; and in the place of reconciliation a grove sprang up, which was named, from the impression which her appearance there made on the luxurious deity, Kamavana, or the wood of desire. The relenting Siva consoled tbe afflicted Rati, the widow of Kama, by assuring her that she should rejoin her husband, when he should be born again in the form of Pradyumna, son of Krishna, and should put Sambara to death.

This favourable prediction was in due time accomplisbed; and Pradyumna was seized by the demon Sambara, who placed him in a chest, and threw it into the sea. The chest was swallowed by a large fish, which was caught and carried, to the palace of the tyrant, wbere the unfortunate Rati had been compelled to menial service; it fell to her lot to open the fish, and finding the chest and its contents, she nursed the infant in private, and educated him until he had sufficient strength to destroy the malignant Sambara. He had before considered Rati as his mother, but their minds being now irradiated, the prophetic promise of Mahadeva was remembered, and the god of love was reunited to the goddess of pleasure

Kamadeva is merely the god of love or desire. Makara-ketu alludes of the fish, Makara, in his banner; Ketu, is the banner. Kandarpa means love, and Kandarpa-ketu is another of his name. Pushpa-dhanva, with the flowery bow. Mara. Ananga, the incorporeal. Madan, and Madamat are names derived, I imagine, from a root signifying both sweetness and toxic potion; honey is called madhu, so is intoxication.

In the beautiful pastoral drama of Jayadeva, called *Gita Govinda*, allusions frequently occur to Kama and his attributes. Radha is thus described bewailing the absence of her beloved Krishna:

"Fresh arrows of desire are continually assailling her, and she forms a net of lotus leaves as armour for her heart, which thou, O Krishna! alone shouldst fortify. She makes her own bed of the arrows darted by the flower-shafted god; but when she hoped for thy embrace, she had formed for thee a couch of their soft blossoms. She draws thy image with musk in the character of the deity with live shafts, having subdued the Makara, and holding an arrow tipped with an amra flower."

Kama's five arrows are eaeh tipped with the blossom of a flower, which is devoted to, and supposcd to preside over, a sense: the flowers are of a heating, inflaming quality; and are named, and well described, in these lines of the hymn, which paint Vasanta preparing the bow and shafts for his mischievous friend:

He bends the lusclous cane, and twists the string
With bees, how sweet! but, ah! how keen their sting
He with five flowerets ties thy ruthless darts,
Which through five senses pierce enraptur'd heart:
Strong Champa, rich in odo'rous gold;
Warm Amer, nurs'd in heavenly mould;
Dry Nagkesar, in silver smiling:

Hot Kitticum, our sense beguiling;
And last, to kiodle fierce the scorching flame,
Lovereft, which gods bright Bela name,"

Among a refined people, advantageously situated in a low latitude, we naturally expect to find love, in its vast variety of relations, no inconsiderable portion of their occupation and amusement. Books and tales on amatory topics are very abundant; and, in common life, allusions are constantly occasions to Kama and his excitations.

On the 13th and 14th of the first half of the month of Chaitra, which must be about the full moon, a festive jollity, with music and bathing, is held in honour of Kamadeva; on which occasion, the following is a popular canticle:

"Hail, god of the flowery bow; hail, warrior, with a fish on thy banner; hail, powerful divinity, who causeth the firmness of the sage to forsake him, and subduest the guardian deities of the eight regions.

"O Kandarpa! thou son of Madhava! O Mara! thou foe of Sambara! Glory be to thee, who lovest the goddess Rati; who springest from the heart!

"Glory be to Madana; to Kama; to him who is formed as the God of gods; to him, by whom Brahma, Vishnu, Siva, Indra, are filled with emotions of rapture!

"May all my mental cares be removed! all my corporeal sufferings terminate! May the object of my soul be attained, and my" (and, gentle reader, thy) *"felicity continue for ever."*

• • •

11

Hanuman, Pavana, Ravana and Garuda

Hanuman

The honour of being the father of Hanuman is claimed by Siva, and by Pavana; the latter is the regent of winds, and, lord or governor, more especially of the north-west quarter of the heavens. To explain this joint concern in the paternity of Hanuman, I will briefly relate a legend from the *Ramayana*.

King Dasaratha, though he had three queens, was childless. To serve this purpose, he was given three cakes by Vasistha, to be fed to the queens after certain ceremonies. He gave one cake to each of his three wives. The third, named Kaikeyi, knowing herself the youngest and favourite wife, was pettish and chagrined that she had not been the first complimented by her lord and looking disdainfully on it, as she held the *pind* (ball) of promise in her hand, a kite made a stoop, and carried it off. Grievously afflicted at this, she gave way to grief and lamentation, which moved her two kind sharers to give her each half of their better-guarded cakes.

Regarding the ravished cake, it is related, that a married Brahmani, named Anjani, being childless, had piously performed supplication and sacrifice to Mahadeva, which so extorted the favour of the generative deity, Rudra, that he promised her an incomparable offspring; and directed her to fix her eyes in profound attention on the sun, holding upward the palms of her hands, and to eat up any substance that might, heaven-directed, fall therein. The cake that the kite had borne off fell in, and she ate it as ordered, and became pregnant; and in due season was delivered of a son, of such surpassing prowess, that at his birth he ground to powder a large stone that happened to be near. This child was Hanuman.

The surprising boy, the immediate offspring of Mahadeva's favour—rather, indeed, the Deva himself, incarnate—became immediately hungry; and his desires were commensurate with the magnificence of his origin; for he longed for the rosy radiance of the then rising sun, in lien of the ordinary nourishment provided for him by nature and his mother; and the demand for this uncommon food, induced the vigorous boy himself to seek it: and he accordingly flew, like the wind, to seize the Surya who, affrighted at the bold attempt, fled; pursued by Hanuman, to the abode of Indra. The god of thunder, launched his ever-ready vajra and smote the audacious chaser in the mouth and felled him almost lifeless to the earth.

Hanuman

Pavana

The share that Pavana had in the production of Hanuman appears to be confined to this: that he comminssioned a Marut, one of his subjects, to guard the dubious cake falling from the kite's beak, and to convey it with happy exactness into the hands of Anjani; and hence Hanuman is called Maruti, the offspring of Marut, a name of Pavana or Vayu, all meaning Wind.

Pavana, afficted and offended at his son's mishap, revenged himself by giving Indra and all the gods the colic: he inflated them to their fullest stretch and closed their breathing orifices to a most painful pitch; until the Devas consented to the restoration of Marut; to whom Indra granted immortality, Surya glory, Chandra celerity, Kuvera wealth, etc., etc. Maruti, however, retained the cleft in his face, given him by Indra's never-failing vajra.

Of Pavan, or Vayu, I have to say, he is, as often mentioned, also called Marut, all names meaning the Wind of which he is the personfication, or regent: he is likewise called Anila, and is sometimes represented mounted on an antelope, to mark his aerial celerity, with a sabre in his hand denoting his energy and acuteness.

Of the regent of the Wind it is related, that, unable to seduce the hundred peerless daughters of Kushanabha, "in beauty of form unparalleled through the earth," begat on Ghritachi, a celestial courtesan, he affected them by a curvature of the spine. "Seeing these

Pavana, God of Wind, with Hanuman in his Lap

damsels one day in the garden, appearing like the stars among clouds, endowed with youth and beauty, and possessed of every accomplishment, Vayu pervading all, thus addressed them: "I entreat you all be espoused to me, abandon the nature of man, and you shall obtain the blessing of longevity. Among mortals, youth is a transitory thing: possessed of unfading youth, you shall obtain immortality."

Incensed at the decorous and dutiful reply, which they concluded by saying, "Our father is our chief deity to whosoever he shall give us, him only will we espouse," the divine Vayu entering them, broke all their bodies. Thus broken, the damsels, overwhelmed with astonishment the house of the king their father and shame in their eyes suffused with tears, entered.

Their admiring father replied: "O daughters! you have acted nobly: forbearance is the great ornament of woman and of man; it is scarcely to be found even among the gods. O that forbearance like yours, O daughters, were passessed by all women; forbearance is generosity; forbearance is truth; forbearance is sacrifice; it is fame; it is virtue." The sequel of this tale shows the moral to be the efficacy of patience.

During the war of Lanka, Rama and a great part of his army were rendered insensible by the potency of certain magical weapons; the effects of which could be removed only by the application of a certain herb before the next rising of the moon. This herb was not a native of the southern parts of India—indeed it grew only on a particular hill in the north, thither Hanuman repaired, with inconceivable celerity; and arriving at the hill, called Devagiri, proceeded, as advised, to seek the shrub, which was to be particularised by a lamp under it; but Hanuman was sorely perplexed at finding a lamp under every shrub and tree on the hill, placed there by the advice of the malignant Indra.

Enraged at being thus baffled, he indignantly tore up the whole mountain, and poised it in one hand. Passing over the city of Ayodhya, the rapidity of his movements caused much concussion in the air; and Bharata, Rama's half-brother, supposing it to proceed from some spirit of darkness, let fly an arrow, and brought Hanuman and his ponderous burden to the ground; but seeing his mistake, offered, in view to the urgency of Hanuman, speedy return, to launch him on an arrow in an instant to Lanka; which mode of conveyance was declined by Hanuman, who proceeded on his journey as before; but some time having been lost by the accident of his fall, he perceived, from his elevation, the refracted rays of the rising moon; and to avert the fatal consequence of being so forestalled, he hid Chandra in his mouth; and thus arriving in time, revivified Rama, Lakshman, and their astounded associates.

Hanuman has appeared several times in my pictures, in one he is assisted by Sugriva, and his associates building the bridge of rocks for the passage of Rama's army in the war of Lanka. Some accounts make the mighty monkey, Nala, son of the divine architect, Viswakarma, the builder of this bridge. Sugriva, the son of Surya, seems the next in rank to Hanuman in this extraordinay army; he is in great favour with Rama. Bali, the son of Indra, having usurped Sugriva's kingdom, they fought a desperate battle, and Bali was afterwards killed by Rama, who reinstated his friend. Hanuman conveyed on his extended arms, Rama and Sita to wherever they went.

Ravana

Ravana, the name meaning tyrant, is also called Dasagriva, the ten-necked; and Pulastya; and Visravan, as son of Visrava, the father also of Kuvera. His numerous heads, and his twenty hands, are the usual symbols of dominion and strength. It is said, in the *Ramayana*, that "where Ravana remains, the Sun loses his force; the winds cease to blow; the fire ceases to burn; the rolling ocean, seeing him, stills its waves." For his predestined destruction Vishnu became incarnate in the person of Rama; and the events leading to it form the story of the *Ramayana*, wherein unity of action is said to be strictly observed. Ravana is styled lord of Rakshashas, malignant beings; many specific varieties of which are enumerated in the first section of the first book of the poem, aiding him in defence of himself and his kingdom of Lanka. They are a marvellous ill-

Ravana and Hanuman

looking set; in many of my pictures painted green, blue, and red, and, engaged in fierce contests with Rama's monkeys. Several legions of these demons, each of 14,000, commanded by Surpanakha, Khara, Dushana, Trishira, etc., were, with their leaders, destroyed by Rama.

Ravana obtained his potency by the usual process of self-inflicted severities; and so ardent was he that he offered to Siva nine of his ten heads successively, and so extorted the favour of the condescendng deity, that, pleased with such an important sacrifice, he promised to grant, with some stipulations, whatever the rigid devotee should desire. The Devatas, alarmed, besought Siva to recall his word; but such conduct is deemed unbecoming in deities, who, however, do not scruple to evade the performance of their promises by some deceit of prevarication; and Siva deputed Narada to sound Ravana as to what he would demand, which as usual was universal dominion. Narada artfully persuaded Ravana that Mahadeva had been drunk, and had promised him what he could not perform; whereupon the vindictive giant tears up Kailasa, the Paradise of Siva; which being contrary to the stipulations, releases Siva from his promise, and he consents to the destruction of Ravana; which is brought about by the Avatara of Rama.

Ravana, by his power and infernal arts, had subjugated all the gods and demigods and forced them to perform menial offices about his person and household. Indra made garlands of flowers to adorn him withal; Agni was his cook; Surya supplied light by day, and Chandra by night; Varuna purveyed water for the palace; Kuvera furnished cash; the whole Navagraha (the nine planetary spheres) for some time arranged themselves into a ladder, by which, they serving as steps, the tyrant ascended his throne; Brahma (for the great gods were there also) was a herald, proclaiming the giant's titles, the day of the week, month. etc., daily in the palace— a sort of speaking almanac; Mahadeva performed the office of barber, and trimmed the giant's beard; Vishnu had the honourable occupation of instructing and drilling the dancing and singing girls, and selecting the fairest for the royal bed; Ganesa had the care of the cows, goats, and herds; Vayu swept the house; Yama washed the linen; and in this manner were all the gods employed in the menial offices of Ravana, who rebuked and flogged them in default of industry and attention. Nor were the female divinities exempted; for Bhavani, in her name and form of Satwi, was head Ayah, or nurse, to Ravana's children; Lakshmi and Saraswati were also among them, but it does not appear in what capacity, Earthly kings and queens were likewise forced into the service of Ravana, to the number of ninety-six royal families, as is said to be detailed in the *Ramayana*.

Such a godly predicament seems essential to the action of Rama, who took immediate and energetic measures for the relief and liberation of the degraded divinities.

Garuda

This animal, half-bird half-man, is the 'vahan or vehicle of Vishnu, and is very frequently introduced into the pictures of the Vaishnavas carrying the deity, with or without Lakshmi; by their sectarists, Krishna and Rama, identified with the preserving power, are sometimes mounted on this vehicle of their archetype. In a picture we see Vishnu and Lakshmi, lotus-seated, on the back of Garuda, whose celerity is proverbial, cleaving the air.

In the picture Garuda has a red comb and beak; his robe is red; his face, arms, legs and pinions, green; the feathers of his wings and tail, green and blue. The sun is seen rising in a very beautiful style over a mountain forming the background; beneath is a river with the lotus floating in it, and aquatic birds are sporting on its banks. Green, red, and blue, are the predominant colours in pictures of Garuda, of which I have many; and there are some points in family and character of this cherub, or man-eagle, indicating that he is a personification of the Sky, the ethereal vehicle of Vishnu as the Sun.

Garuda is the son of Vinata, and hence called Vinateya; Vinata, sometimes called Vinava, is his mother, Kasyapa being his father. The all-prolific Diti is occasionally spoken of as Garuda's mother; and he is brother to Aruna, or Aurora. Tarksha, Garutwanta, Suparna, and Punagri are other names of Garuda; he has other epithets equivalent to foe of serpents, or their destroyer, Nagantaka;

Garuda, named Jatayu, with Rama on its back

favourite bird of Hari; lord of birds; swift as wind; and he is generally spoken of, in a strain of praise, as being generous and merciful. The name Suparna is derived, I believe, from the beauty of his plumage.

He gives a name to a Purana, wherein his genealogy and exploits are detailed. He had a son of some note, named Sunabha; and his sister, Sumati, a maid of surpassing beauty as her name implies, was espoused by Sagara, king of Ayodhya.

He was of great use to Krishna in clearing the country around Dwarka from savages, ferocious animals, and noxious reptiles. Vishnu had granted to Garuda the power of destroying his, as well as Siva's, enemies; also generally those guilty of constant uncleanness, unbelievers, dealers in iniquity, ungrateful persons, those who slander their spiritual guides, or defiled their beds; but forbade him to touch a Brahmin, whatever was his guilt, as the pain of disobedience would be scorching flame in his throat, and any attack on a holy or pious person would be followed by a great diminution of strength.

By mistake, however, Garuda sometime seized a priest, or a religious man, but was admonished and punished in the first case by the scorching flame , and was unable even when he had bound him in his den to hurt the man of piety. To Rama also in the war of Lanka, Garuda was eminently useful: in Rama's last conflict with Ravana, the latter was not overcome without the aid of Garuda, sent by Vishnu to destroy the serpent-arrows of Ravana. These arrows are called Sarpa-vana, and had the faculty of separating, between the bow and the object, into many parts, each becoming a serpent. Viswamitra conferred upon Rama the power of transforming his arrows into Garuda-vanas, they similarly separating themselves into Garuda's, the terror and destroyer of the Sarpa.

Some legends make Garuda the offspring of Kasyapa and Diti. This all prolific dame laid an egg, which, it was predicted, would produce her deliverer from some great atlliction; after a lapse of five hundred years, Garuda sprung from the egg, flew to the abode of Indra, extinguished the fire that surrounded it, conquered its guards, the devatas, and bore off the Amrita which enabled him to liberate his captive mother. A few drops of this immortal beverage falling on the species of grass called Kusa, it became eternally consecrated; and the serpents greedily licking it up, so lacerated the tongues with the sharp grass, that they have ever since remained forked; but the boon of eternity was ensured to them by their thus partaking of the immortal fluid. This curse of snakes having forked tongues is still popularly, in the tales of India, attributed to the above greediness; and their supposed immortality may have originated in some such stories as these: a small portion of Amrita, as in the case of Rahu, would ensure them this boon.

The swan, or goose, the eagle, and the bull, are the vehicles respectively allotted to the three great powers. The terrestrial sluggish nature of the first, I have supposed, pointed it out as an apt type of matter, personified in the appropriately mounted on the buoyant eagle, the celestial Garuda. Siva, the destructive energy of the Deity, is Time, or Justice; and the Hindus, but deem the bull also its type, and give it to Siva as his vahan, or mode of conveyance. These vehicles are supposed by Mr. Paterson to have allusion to "Purity, Truth, and Justice" the first, typified by the swan, which, clothed with unspotted whiteness, swims amidst the waters, as it were, distinct from, and unsullied by them; as the truly pure mind remains untainted amidst the surrounding temptations of the world. Justice is typified in the sacred bull, the vahan of Siva: "the bull, whose body is Parameswara, and whose every joint is a virtue; whose three horns are the three Vedas; whose tail ends where Adharma, or injustice, begins."

• • •

12

Hindu Scriptures

There are eighteen Vidyas, or parts, of true knowledge, and some branches of knowledge, falsely so called.

The first four are the immortal Vedas, evidently revealed by God; which are entitled, in one compound word, Rigyajussamatharva, or, in separate words, Rig, Yajush, Sama and Atharva, The Rigveda consists of five schools, the Yajurveda of eighty-six, the Samaveda of a thousand, and the Atharvaveda of nine; with eleven hundred Sakhas, or branches, in various divisions and subdivisions.

From these are deduced the four Upavedas; namely, Ayush, Gandharva, Dhanur, and Sthapatya. The first of which, or Ayurveda, was delivered to mankind by Brahma, Indra, Dhanwantari, and five other deities; and comprises the theory of disorder and medicines, with the practical methods of curing diseases. The second, on music, was invented and explained by Bharata: it is chiefly useful in raising the mind by devotion to the felicity of the Divine Nature. The third Upaveda was composed by Viswamitra, on the fabrication and use of arms, and implements handled in war by Kshatriyas. Viswakarman revealed the fourth, in various treatises on sixty-four mechanical arts, for the improvement of such as exercise them.

Six Angas, or bodies of learning, are also derived from the same source; their subjects chiefly are: 1. pronunciation of vocal sounds; 2. detail of religious acts and ceremonies; 3. grammar; 4. prosody; 5. astronomy; and 6, signification of difficult words and phrases in the Vedas.

Lastly, there are four Upangas called, Purana, Nyaya, Mimansa, and Dharma-sastra. Eighteen puranas (that of Brahma, and the rest) were composed by Vyasa, for the instruction and entertainment of mankind in general. Nyaya is a collection of treatises, in two parts, on metaphysics, logic, philosophy, etc. Mimansa is somewhat similar, divided into two parts; the latter, called Uttara, abounding in questions on the Divine Nature and other sublime speculations, was composed by Vyasa, in four chapters and sixteen sections. It may be considered as the brain and spring of all the Angas; it exposes the heretical opinions of sophists; and in a manner suited to the comprehension of adepts, it treats on the true nature of Ganesa, Bhaskara, or the Sun, Nilakanta, Lakshmi and other forms of One Divine Being.

Worship Vase of Gilt Bronze

The body of Law called Smriti, consists of eighteen books, delivered for the instruction of the human species, by Manu and other sacred personages.

As to ethics, the Vedas contain all that relates to the duties of kings; the Puranas, what belong to the relation of husband and wife; and the duties of friendship and society, which complete the triple division.

The *Mahabharata* and *Ramayana*, both epic poems, comprise the most valuable part of ancient history.

Sankhya is twofold—told with Iswara, and that without Iswara; called Patanjali and Kapila; the latter, in six chapters, on the production of all things by the union of Prakriti, or Nature, and Purusha, or the first male, etc.

The Mimansa is in two parts, the Nyaya in two and the Sankhya in two; and these six schools comprehend all the doctrines of the theists.

There are also six atheistical systems of philosophy, entitled Yogachara, Saudhanta, Vaibhashika, Madhyamika, Digambara and Charvak, all full of indeterminate phrases, errors in sense, confusion between distinct qualities, incomprehensible notions, opinions not duly weighed and tenets destructive of natural equality—containing a jumble of athesim and ethics; distributed, like our orthodox books, into a number of sections, which omit what ought to be omitted; abounding in false propositions, idle propositions, and impertinent propositions.

Such is the analysis of unversal knowledge, practical and speculative.

A very ingenious and learned commentary, by Sir William Jones is as follows:

"The Vedas consist of three Kandas, or general heads—namely, Karma, Jnana, and Upasana; or works, faith and worship. To the first of which, the author of the *Vidyadarsa*, or view of learning, a rare Sanskrit book, wisely gives the preference; as Manu himself prefers universal benevolence to the ceremonies of religions.

"After all the books on divine knowldege called the Veda, or what is known, and Sruti, or what has been heard, from revelation, are still supposed to be very numerous; and the four here mentioned are thought to have been selected as containing all the information necessary for man.

"From the Vedas are immediately deduced the practical arts of surgery and medicine; music and dancing; archery, which comprises the whole art of war; and architecture, under which the system of mechanical arts is included.

"Next in order to these, are the six Vedangas; three of which belong to grammar; one relates to religious cermonies; a fifth, to the whole compass of mathematics; and the sixth, to the explanation of obscure words or phrases in the Vedas.

"Subordinate to these Angas are the series of sacred poems, the body of law, and the six philosophical sastras.

"The first Indian poet was Valmiki, author of the *Ramayana*, a complete epic poem, on one continued, interesting, and heroic action; and the next in celebrity, if it be not superior to it in reputation for holiness, is the *Mahabharat* of Vyasa. To him are ascribed the sacred Puranas, which are eighteen and which have the following titles: 1. Brahma, or the Great One, 2. Padma, or the lotus, 3. Brahmanda, or the mundane egg, 4. Agni, or fire (these four relate to creation), 5. Vishnu, or the pervader; 6 Garuda, or his eagle; 7. the tranformations of Brahma, 8. Siva, 9. Linga, 10, Narada, son of Brahma, 11. Skanda, son of Siva, 12. Markandeya, or the immortal man, 14 Bhavishya, or the prediction of futurity (these nine belong to the attributes and powers of the deity), 14. Matsya; 15. Varaha, 16. Kurma; 17. Vamana, or as many incarnations of the great one in his character of preserver—all containing ancient traditions, embellished by poetry, or disguised by fable. The eighteenth is the *Bhagavata* or life of Krishna, with which the same poet is by some imagined to have crowned the whole series, though others, with more reason, assign them differnt composers.

"Of the philosophical schools it will be sufficient here to remark, that the Nyaya seems analagous to the peripatetic; the second, sometimes called Vaisheshika, to the Ionic; the two Mimansas, of which the second is often distinguished by the name of Vedanta, to the Platonic; the first Sankhya, to the Italic, and the second, or Patanjali, to the Stoic, philosophy.

"It results, from this analysis of Hindu literature, that the Veda, Upaveda, Vedanga, Purana, Dharma, and Darsana, are the six great Sastras, in which all knowledge, divine and human, is supposed to be comprehended. And here we must not forget, that the word Sastra, derived from a root signifying to ordain means generally an ordinance, and particularly a sacred ordinance delivered by inspiration; properly, therefore, the word is applied only to sacred literature, of which the text exhibits an accurate sketch.

"Wherever we direct our attention to Hindu literature, the notion of infinity presents itself; and the longest life would not be sufficient for the perusal of nearly five hundred thousand stanzas in the Puranas, with a million more, perhaps in the other works before mentioned. We may however select the best from each Sastra, and gather the fruits of science, without loading ourselves with the leaves and branches; while we have the pleasure to find that the learned Hindus, encouraged by the mildness of our government and manners, are at least as eager to communicate their knowledge of all kinds as we can be to receive it. But if we wish to form a correct idea of Indian religion and literature, let us begin by forgetting all that has been wrtitten on the subject by ancients or moderns before the publication of the *Gita*."

Some further particulars on the subject of the Vedas and Puranas, according to Mr. Colebrooke, are:

"The Hindus believe that the original Veda was revealed by Brahma, and to have been preserved by tradition until it was arranged in its present form by a sage, who thence obtained the name of Vyasa, or Veda Vyasa, that is compiler of the Vedas. He distributed the Indian scripture into four parts, which are severally entitled Rik, Yajush, Saman and Atharvana, and each of which bears the common denomination of Veda.

"With the Hindus it is an article of their creed, that the Vedas were composd by no human author. It must be understood, therefore, that in affirming the primeval existence of their scriptures, they deny these works to be the original composition of the editor, Vyasa, but believe them to have been gradually revealed to inspired writers.

"The Vedas are compilation of prayers, called Mantras; with collection of precepts and maxims, entitled Brahmana; from which last portion the Upanishad is extracted. The prayers are properly the Vedas and apparently preceded the Brahmana.

"Each Veda consists of two parts, denominated the Mantras and the Brahmanas, or prayer and precepts. The complete collection of the hymns, prayers, and invocations, belonging to one Veda, is entitled its Samhita; every other portion of Indian scriptures is included under the general head of divinity — Brahmana—this comprises precepts which inculcate religious duties, maxims which explain those precepts, and arguments which relate to theology. But in the present arrangement of the Vedas, the portion which contains passages called Brahmana, includes many which are strictly prayers or Mantras. The theology of the Indian scripture, comprehending the argumentative portion entitled Vedanta, is contained in tracts denominated Upanishad; some of which are portions of the Brahmana, properly so called; others are found only in a detached form; and one is a part of a Samhita itself.

"Prayers employed at solemn rites, called Yajnas, have been placed in the three principal Vedas: those which are in prose are named Yajush; such as are in metre, are denominated Rik and some which are intended to be chanted, are called Saman; and those names as distinguishing different portions of the

Vedas, are anterior to their separation in Vyasa's compilation. But the Atharvana, not being used at the religious ceremonies above mentioned, and containing prayers employed at lustrations, at rites conciliating the deities, and as imprecations on enemies is essentially differnt from the other Vedas.

"Every Purana treats of five subjects: 1. the creation of the universe, 2. its progress and the renovation of worlds, 3. the genealogy of gods and heroes, 4. chronology according to a fabulous system and 5. heroic history containing the achievements of demigods and heroes. Since each Purana contains a cosmogony, with mythological and heroic history the works which bear that title may not inaptly be compared to the Grecian Theogonies.

"The subjects and uses of the prayers contained in the Vedas differ more than the deities which are invoked, or the titles by which they are addressed: every line is replete with allusions to mythology and to the Indian notions of the Divine Nature and of celestial spirits. For the innumerable ceremonies to be performed by a householder, and, still more for those endless rites enjoined to hermits and ascetics, a choice of prayers is offered in every stage of the celebration. It may be here sufficient to observe, that Indra or the firmament, fire, the sun, the moon, water, air, the spirits, the atmosphere, and the earth are the objects most frequently addressed; and the various and repeated sacrifices with fire, and the drinking of the milky juice of the moon-plant, or *acid asclepias,* furnish abundant occasions for numerous prayers adapted to the many stages of those religious rites."

The reverence in which the Vedas are held by the Hindus will appear from the following texts in the Book of Manu:

"From fire, from air, and from the sun, he (the Supreme Ruler) milked out, as it were, the three primordial Vedas, named Rik, Yajush, and Saman, for the due performance of the sacrifice.

"The Rigveda is held sacred to the gods; the Yajurveda relates to mankind; the Samaveda concerns the manes of ancestors, and the sound of it, when chanted, raises therefore a notion of something impure.

"Let the learned read the Vedas on every lawful day, having first repeated, in order, the pure essence of the three Vedas, namely, the Pranava, the Vyahritis and Gayatri."

The term Upanishad has frequently occurred, and seems not to have, in general, any accurate idea annexed to it. The proper meaning of the word Upanishad, according to Mr. Colebrooke, is divine science or the knowledge of God; and it is equally applicable to theology itself and to a book in which this science is taught.

The whole of the Indian theology is professedely founded on the Upanishads. Some are extracts from the Vedas; and the rest are also considered as appertaining to the Indian scripture.

The word Sastra, we find to mean, generally, an ordinance, and particularly a sacred ordinance, delivered by inspiration; and properly applicable only to sacred literature.

• • •

13

Sects of the Hindus

That the Hindus belong to various sects is universally known, but their characteristic differences are not perhaps generally understood. Five great sects exclusively worship a single deity. These are:

1. The Saivas who, however, worship Siva and Bhavani conjointly.
2. The Vaishnavas, who worship Vishnu.
3. The Suras, who worship Surya, or the Sun.
4. The Ganapatyas, who worship Ganesa.
5. The Saktas, who exclusively worship Bhavani, the Sakti, or female energy, of Siva.

But if we closely examine the relation they respectively bear to each other, we shall find the 4th and 5th to be subdivisions, or ramifications of the 1st, or 1. Saiva: of which may be traced these distinctions—Siva itself meaning the worshippers of Siva, or of Siva and Parvati conjointly. 2. Lingi, the adorers of Siva, or his Phallic type, separately. 3. Sakti, the adorers of the Yoni of Bhavani, or her symbol, separately. and 4. The Ganapatyas, the exclusive worshippers of Ganesa, the first-born of Mahadeva and Parvati.

The second grand sect of Vaishnavas is variously divided and subdivided.

First, or division of Gokulastha, or worshippers of Gokul. or Krishna, is subdivided into three:

1. Exclusively worship Krishna as Vishnu himself; this is generally deemed the true and orthodox Vaishnava.
2. Exclusively worship Radha as the Sakti of Krishna or Vishnu; this sect is called Radha-vallabhi.
3. Worship Krishna and Radha conjointly.

Second, or division of Ramanuj, or worshippers of Ramachandra, is, in like manner, subdivided into three:

1. Worship Rama only.
2. Worship Sita only as his Sakti.
3. Worship both Rama and Sita conjointly.

One recognises the five divinities which are adored by the other sects respectively; but the followers of this comprehensive scheme mostly select one object of daily devotion, and pay adoration to other deities on particular occasions. Even they deny the charge of polytheism, and repel the imputation of idolatry; they justify the practice of adoring the images of celestial spirits by arguments similar to those which have been elsewhere employed in defence of image worship.

If the doctrines of the Veda, and even those of the Puranas, be closely examined,

For the Vaishnavas, Vishnu is the greatest in the Triad

the Hindu theology will be found consistent monotheism, though it contains the seeds of polytheism and idolatry. Modern Hindus seem to misunder-stand the numerous texts which declare the unity of the Godhead, and the identity of Vishnu, Siva, the Sun, etc. Their theologists have entered into vain disputes on the question, which, among the attributes of God, shall be deemed characteristic and pre-eminent. Sankaracharya, the celebrated commentator, contended for the attributes of Siva; and founded, or confirmed, the sect of Saivas, who worship Mahadeva as Supreme Being, and deny the independent existence of Vishnu and other deities. Madhavacharva, and Vallabhacharya, have, in like manner, established the sect of Vaishnavas, who adore Vishnu as God. The less numerous Suras worship the Sun, and acknowledge no other divinity. The Ganapatyas adore Ganesa as uniting in his person all the attributes of the Deity.

As the Saiva has a fourth undivided sect in the Ganapatyas, so the Vaishnava has a fourth undivided sect in the Bhagavatas. And, indeed, we find the sects melting into each other; for, in consequence of the interposition of Vishnu to appease a physiologicai difference between Mahadeva and Parvati, or the worshippers of the Linga and Yoni, his (Vishnu's) navel came to be considered as the same with the Yoni confounding the Yonijas with the Vaishnavas.

The Hindu mythology has personified the abstract and attractive powers of the

For the Shaivas, Mahadeva is Supreme in the Triad

Divinity, and has ascribed sexes to these mythological personages. The Sakti, or energy, of an attribute of God is female, and fabled as the consort of that personified attribute. The Sakti of Siva, whose emblem is the Phallus, is herself typified by the female organ; this the Saktas worship, some figuratively, others literally.

Vopadeva, the author of *Sri Bhagavata*, has endeavoured to reconcile all the sects of Hindus by reviving the doctrines of Vyasa. He recognises all the deities, but as subordinate to the Supreme Being, or rather as attributes or manifestations of God. A new sect has been thus formed, and is denominated from that modern Purana; but the numerous followers of it do not seem to have well apprehended the doctrines they profess. They incline much to real polytheism, but do at least reject tbe derogatory notions of the Divinity, which the other sects seem to have adopted.

The Vaishnavas, though nominally worshippers of Vishnu, are in fact, votaries of deified heroes. The Gokulasthas, one branch of this sect adore Krishna, while the Ramanuj worship Ramachandra. Both have again branched into three sects: one consists in the exclusive worshippers of Krishna; and these only are deemed true and orthodox Vaishnavas; another joins his favourite Radha with the hero; a third, called Radhavallabhi, adores Radha only, considering her as the active power of Vishnu. The followers of these sects have adopted the singular practice of presenting to their own wives the oblations intended for the goddess; and those among them who follow the Vama or left-handed path (there is in most sects a right-handed, or decent path, and a left-handed, ot indecent mode of worsbip) require their wives to be naked when attending them at their devotions.

Among the Ramanuj some worship Rama only, and others both Rama and Sita; none of them practise any indecent mode of worship. And they all, like the Gokulasthas, as well as the followers of the Bhagavata, delineate on their foreheads a double upright line with chalk, or with sandalwood, and a red circlet with turmeric and lime; but the Ramanuj add an uprlght red line in the middle of the double white one.

The Saivas are all worshippers of Siva and Bhavani conjointly; and they adore the Linga, or the compound type of this god and goddess, as the Vaishnavas do the image of Lakshmi-Narayana. There are no exclusive worshippers of Siva besides the sect of naked gymnosophists, called Lingis; and the exclusive adorers of the goddess are the Saktas. In this last mentioned sect, as in most others, there is a right-handed and decent path, and left-handed indecent mode of worship; but the indecent worship of this sect is most grossly so, and consists of unbridled debauchery with wine and women. This profligate sect is supposed to be numerous, though unavowed. In most parts of India, if not in all, they are held in deserved detestation; and even the decent Saktas do not make public profession of their tenets, nor wear on their foreheads the marks of their sect, lest they should be suspected of belonging to the other branch of it.

The Saivas and Saktas delineate on their foreheads three horizontal lines with ashes, obtained, if possible, from the hearth on which a consecrated fire has been maintained; they add a red circlet, which the Saivas make of red sanders, and which the Saktas, when they avow themselves, mark either with saffron, or with turmeric and borax.

The Sauras are true worshippers of the Sun; and some of them, it seems, adore the dormant and active energies of the planet conjointly. This sect, which is not very numerous, is distinguished by the use of red sanders for the horizontal triple line, as well as for the circlet on their foreheads.

The Ganapatyas have not, so far as I can learn, branched into different sects; nor can I add any information, respecting their peculiar tenets, further than that Ganesa is exclusively worshipped by them. This sect is distinguished by the use of red minium for the circlet on their foreheads.

The left-handed path, or indecent mode of worship, of several sects, especially that of the Saktas, is founded on the Tantras, which are, for this reason, held in disesteem.

• • •

14

Sectarial Marks and Symbols

The Hindus are prone to fancying a type of sometimes mysterious in almost every subject that can come under their contemplation; anything hollowed out, conveying an idea of capacity, they deem typical of the Yoni, or Argha, itself a type of female nature, or the Sakti, or power of Siva. The sea, a pond, a well, a cave, the palm of the hand or anything similarly hollowed, convey to their enthusiastic minds an idea of the Argha; and their peripheri, real or imaginary, an idea of the Yoni. In like manner, a mountain, a hill, a tree deprived of its boughs, a mast, a pole, an obelisk, a pyramid, or anything conical or erect, excites an idea of the Linga; and such subject they can fancy its symbol: a conical stone is particularly so esteemed, or fire, whose natural and necessary form is conical.

Hence a triangle with its apex upwards, is the immediate type of Mahadeva, who, in some relations, is Fire personified—Vishnu is, in like manner, personification of the principle of humidity; and water is symbolized by a cone, or triangle, with its apex downwards; and water is symbolized by a cone, or triangle, with its apex downwards: these types correctly denoting the ascending and descending properties of their respective prototypes—elemental fire and water. The two conjoined express the junction or union of the two elements, or deities; this mark, or character, is said to represent also Vishnu and Prithivi.

The triangle is called Trikon a and has been explained as the symbol of certain deities or powers, and as the type of triune coequality: and hence applied by some to the three great powers conjointly. A circle is Brahman, Eternity; having neither beginning nor end—unity—perfection. A circle enclosing a triangle, and a triangle enclosing a circle, have also mysterious allusions, Trinity in Unity, and Unity in Trinity.

In the Durga-puja, the sacred jar is marked with the combined triangle, denoting the union of the two deities, Siva and Durga. The Saktas, worshippers of the Sakti, or female principle, mark the jar with 65. The Vaishnavas, In their puja, use also a mystical jar, which is marked 71. These marks are called Tantra and are heiroglyphic characters, of which there are a vast number.

The jar is used at festivals, and is consecrated by prayers, invoking the presence of the deity or deities, who are on that occasion worshipped; adding also invocations to Ganga and other holy rivers. When celebration of the festival is completed, the holy water contained

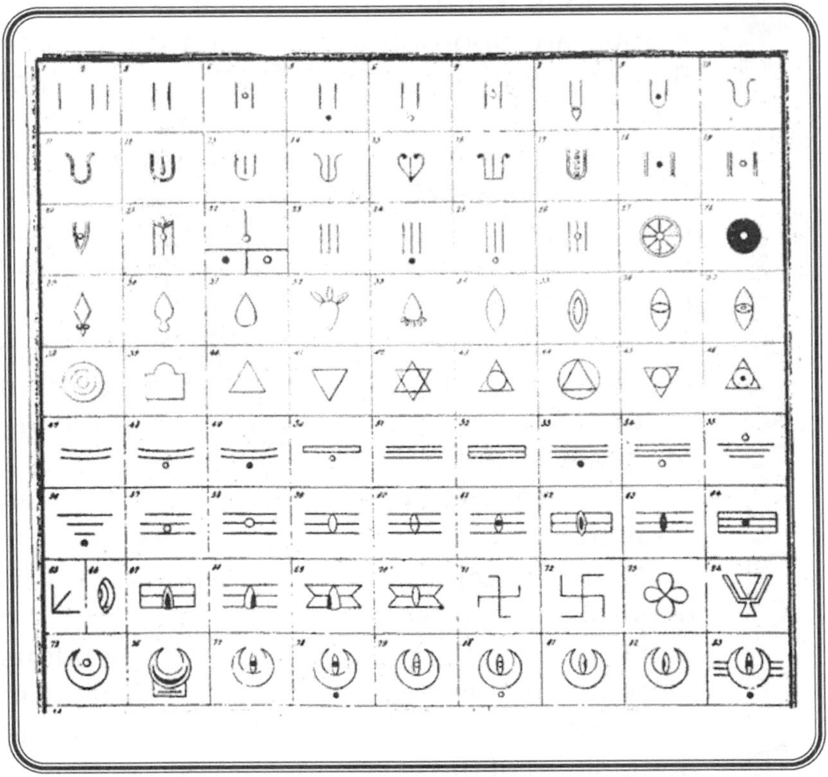

Sectarial Marks and Symbols

in the jar is employed by the priests to sprinkle or bathe the person who commands and defrays the expenses of the celebration.

Various Yantras, or mystical figures and marks, are appropriated to each deity; such figures are usually delineated on the spot where a consecrated jar is to be placed. These Yantras which are supposed by superstitious Hindus to possess occult powers, are taught in great detail by the Tantras, or Agama Sastra; but seem to be unknown to the Vedas and Puranas.

The words Yantra and Tantra, as well as to hieroglyphics, are applied also to a sort of invocatory incantation of a supplicatory tendency—Tantra especially; Yantra means a sort of magic square, either of figures, or an abracadabra.

Mantra is an imprecatory incantation; it is generally composed of a passage from the Veda, in which the names of some tremendous deity occurs. The Hindus have great faith in the efficacy of propitiatory incantations and great dread of those of a malevolent tendency.

The following passage from the *Ramayana* will exemplify this; and, with those who have faith in such works, affords a sufficient reason to fear the effects of such curses:

"Even he who cannot be slain by the ponderous arms of Indra, nor by those of Kali, nor by the terrible chakra of Vishnu, shall be destroyed, if a Brahmin curse him, as if he were consumed by fire."

Worship Materials

It is generally known that Hindus mark their foreheads, and have a superstitious regard for such distinctions. I have been told, that it is held necessary, where convenient, or no especial objection or difficulty exists, for these marks to be daily renewed, and, of course, by the hand of a Brahmin. One of that sect cannot perform any of his daily sacrifices, ablutions. etc., without the completion or contemplation of this distinction; and it is irreverent in one of an inferior tribe to approach a holy man, or to ask his blessing, or to partake in the benefit of any religious rite, without, or in view to, this sectarial decoration.

The race of Hindus are generally understoodz to be divided into the two grand sects of Saiva, otherwise called Sivabhakta, worshippers of Siva; and Vaishnava, otherwise, of Vishnu. These, as has been so often noticed, are variously subdivided; but it is said that the former are to be known by the horizontal position of their forehead lines, and the latter, by their perpendicularity.

One perpendicular mark centrally between the eyes is generally referrable to one of Vishnu's sectaries; it is not common.

Two upright parallel lines, with a black or open circlet between or under them, are the commonest distinction of Vaishnavas, whether seen on pictures of Vishnu himself, or of Rama and Krishna, or others of his Avataras.

Three perpendicular lines, with or without dots or circles, appertain to the sects of Vaishnava, and horizontal lines, to sects of

Saiva. Three upright lines are by no means so common as two. I do not recollect that I ever saw them as forehead marks, either in pictures or on men.

The Saivas and Saktas draw on their foreheads three horizontal lines, with ashes adding a red circlet; the Saktas avow themselves with saffron, or with turmeric. The Sauras are distinguished by the horizontal triple line, as well as the circlet, while the Ganapatyas use red minium for the circlet.

As well as the forehead, it will have been observed that Hindus paint their arms and breasts also, and sometimes their throats; sandal powder, turmeric, chuna, or lime, ashes from a consecrated fire, cow-dung, and other holy combustibles, made adhesive by a size of rice-water, or sometimes rubbed on dry, are the ingredients and usages on this occasion. Several lines of white, ashen, or yellow hue, are commonly seen drawn across the arms and breasts; and I understand that Yogis and Sanyasis, and other pious persons, frequently carry about them a little packet of these holy pigments, with which they mark those who show them respect, in repayment of their attentions.

The extreme importance that the Hindus attach to the supposed profundity of the Gayatri, render it a text of more curiosity than, perhaps, indifferent readers will be able to discover in the words themselves, in either their familiar or recondite allusions.

I shall give several translations of it, by different Sanskrit scholars, premising that it is a text mentally recited, never articulated.

Sir W. Jones says that the Gayatri is called the "Mother of the Vedas."

"The many panegyrics on the Gayatri, the Mother, as it is called, of the Vedas, prove the author to have adored, not the visible material sun, but that divine and incomparably greater light, which illumines all, delights all, from which all proceed, to which all must return, and which alone can irradiate not our visual organs merely, but our souls, and our intellects. These may be considered as the words of the most venerable text in the Indian scripture."

Another translation occurs in the thirteenth volume of his work, in which the author seemed to intend making the translation as literal as possible:

"The Gayatri, or holiest verse of the Vedas.

"Let us adore the supremacy of that divine Sun, the Godhead who illuminates all, who recreates all, from whom all proceed, to whom all must return; whom we invoke to direct our understandings aright in our progress toward his holy seat."

The following parapbrase, or commentary, is by a learned Pandit, and is evidentiy descriptive of Brahma:

"Perfect truth; perfect happiness; without equal; immortal; absolute unity; whom neither speech can describe, nor mind comprehend;

all-pervading; all-transcending; delighted with his own boundless intelligence; not limited by space or time; without feet, moving swiftly; without hands, grasping all worlds; without eyes, all-surveying; without ears, all-hearing; without an intelligent guide, understanding all; without cause, the first of all causes; all-ruling; all-powerful; the creator, preserver, transformer, of all things.—Such is the Great One: this the Vedas declare."

According to Manu—"Brahma milked out, as it were, from the three Vedas, the letter A, the letter U, and the letter M; together with three mysterious words, *bhur, bhuvah, swah*; or earth, sky, heaven.

"From the three Vedas also, the Lord of Creatures, incomprehensibly exalted, successively milked out the three treasures of that ineffable text, beginning with the word Tad, and entitled Savitri, or Gayatri.

"A priest who shall know the Veda, and shall pronounce to himself, both morning and evening, that syllable, and that holy text, preceded by the three words, shall attain the sanctity which the Veda confers.

"And a twice-born man, who shall a thousand times repeat those three (Om, the Vyahritis, and the Gayatri) apart from the multitude, shall be released in a month even from a great offence, as a snake from his slough.

"The priest, the soldier and the merchant, who shall neglect this mysterious text, and fail to perform in due season his peculiar acts of piety, shall meet with contempt among the virtuous.

"The three great immutable words, preceded by the triliteral syllable, and followed by the Gayatri, which consists of three measures, must be considered as the mouth, or principal part of the Veda.

"Whoever shall repeat, day by day, for three years, without negligence, that sacred text, shall hereafter approach the divine essence, move as freely as air, and assume an ethereal form.

"By the sole repetition of the Gayatri, a priest may indubitably attain beatitude, let him perform or not perform any other religious act.

"Even three suppressions of breath, made according to the divine rule, accompanied by the triverbal phrase (*bhurbhuvaswah*), and the triliteral syllable (Om), may be considered as the highest devotion of a Brahmin;

"For as the dross and impurities of metallic ores are consumed by fire, thus are the sinful acts of the human organ consumed by the suppression of the breath, while the mystic words and the measures of the Gayatri are revolved in the mind."

In another place, thus renders the important:

"Earth! Sky! Heaven!—Let us meditate on thee, and on the most excellent light and power of that generous, sportive, and resplendent Sun; praying that it may guide our intellects."

The last hymn, or Sukta, of the third book of the first Veda, which book contains invocations by Viswamitra, consists of six prayers; one of which includes the celebrated Gayatri. This remarkable text is repeated more than once in other Vedas; but since Viswamitra is the Rishi to whom it was revealed, it appears that its proper and original place is in this hymn.

Sayanacharya considers this passage to admit of two interpretations: The light, or Brahman, constituting the splendour of the Supreme Ruler, or the Creator of the Universe; or the light, or orb, of the splendid Sun.

The sacred monosyllable is generally spelled Om; but being triliteral, seems better expressed by Aum, or Aom, or Awm, it being formed of the three Sanskrit letters that are best so represented. This mystic emblem of the Deity is forbidden to be pronounced but in silence. "The first letter stands tor the Creator, the second for the Preserver, and the third for the Destroyer."

Again: "Om. Tat, and Sat," are the three mystic characters used to denote the Deity. The word Tat is used for qualities which are true, and for qualities which are holy: it is applied also to deeds which are praiseworthy. Attention in worship, zeal, and deeds of charity, are likewise called Sat.

Krishna, describing his own excellences, selects the first and best of many things to compare to himself. "I am," he says to Arjun, "the monosyllable among words. Amongst harmonious measures, I am the Gayatri."

This mystic sign of Brahman is also known by the name of Pranava and by making a sort of double cypher of the Om, and filling it up, and giving a body to the central and connecting part of the cypher, fancies he has discovered a mysterious triad represented at Jagannath.

This word, used like our Amen, at the end of prayers, is used also at their beginning. It also expresses a sound not very different from Amen.

• • •

Other Books on
PHILOSOPHY, RELIGION & CULTURE

1. My Experiments With Truth **(New)**
2. Gandhi Global For The New Gen **(New)**
3. The Golden Book of World Religions **(New)**`
4. Hindu Social System First Famous Study
5. The Lotus Sutra Saddharma Pundarika
6. The Master Swami Vivekananda
7. Everyman's Book of Hindu Religion & Mythology
8. The ABC of Hindu Culture
9. India in China The Gift of Buddha
10. The Vital Truths of Hinduism
11. Philosophy India
12. The Dhammapada
13. The Last Days of Lord Buddha
14. Complete Book of Hindu Gods And Goddesses
15. Vatsyayana's Kamasutra Select and his times
16. The Kama Sutra of Mallinaga Vatsyayana
17. Judgment NoAircrash NoDeath
18. Patriot Netaji Subhas Chandra Bose
19. The Life of Lord Buddha
20. The Discourses of Lord Buddha
21. The Golden Book of Buddhism
22. The Golden Book of Hinduism
23. The Golden Book of Islam
24. The Golden Book of Rigveda
25. The Golden Book of Jainism

26. The Golden Book of Upanishads
27. Learn Rajayoga from Vivekananda
28. Colossus Vivekananda Select
29. Intellect India
30. Culture India
31. Mahatma Gandhi The Bhagavadgita
32. Shirdi Sai Baba
33. The Ramayana For Every Home **(New)**
34. The Mahabharata For Every Home **(New)**
35. Sai - The Age of Cosmic Family
36. Sathya Sai and His Miraculous Powers
37. To Bloom Like a Lotus
38. The History of Sikh Gurus
39. Indian Mythology
40. Human Rights in Islam

Lotus PRESS
Unit No. 220, 2nd Floor, 4735/22, Prakash Deep Building,
Ansari Road, Darya Ganj, New Delhi- 110002
Ph.: 41325510, 9811838000
• E-mail : lotuspress1984@gmail.com, www.lotuspress.co.in